Dear Adi

Come, Walk With Me

A Life Lived With Joy

May you have

abundant Joy!

Edith Matthies

Edith Adrian Matthies

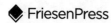 FriesenPress

Suite 300 - 990 Fort St
Victoria, BC, V8V 3K2
Canada

www.friesenpress.com

Book Cover Design: John Zacharias

Content Editor: Denny M. Smith

Illustrator: Breanna Froese

ISBN
978-1-5255-1542-2 (Hardcover)
978-1-5255-1543-9 (Paperback)
978-1-5255-1544-6 (eBook)

1. BIOGRAPHY & AUTOBIOGRAPHY, RELIGIOUS

Distributed to the trade by The Ingram Book Company

TABLE OF CONTENTS

FOREWORD

Come Walk With Me, A Life Lived With Joy invites the reader into the memories of a woman who has the capacity to look backwards even as she gazes toward the evening horizon of her life. Those head-turning reflections will elicit smiles, and even audible laughter. The reader will find them poignant, thought provoking and deeply personal.

The faces of "all" people, as the author has shared life with them, are faces of all ages, of all stations in life, and of all relationships with our Maker. One face that pervades all of the text is the face of God.

This is a work of love that disrobes the soul of a woman of God. The reader is permitted to observe the inner life of an ordinary person described as being: intellectually blessed, emotionally alive with an infectious laugh, transparently faithful, agonizingly aware of feet of clay, mother and daughter, wife and best friend, openly repentant, uncertain in some things; but absolutely certain in others.

It has been said that most of our life is spent, not in the lowest or the highest moments; it is spent in the middle. This book is an expression of salvation as understood this way. It is a record of a life in the middle, in the middle of all the joys and fears, the chuckles, and the second thoughts that attend the life of faithful Christians.

Come Walk With Me, A Life Lived With Joy is an invitation to walk with someone whose deepest desire is to be a faithful lover of God.

-Denny M. Smith

JOY:

- *a state of being*
- *an intentional choice of perspective*
- *produced by the Holy Spirit*
- *a command of God*

Father, command what You will of me,
and grant me what you command.
—St. Augustine

(So, God, I know You're telling me to be joyful, but,
I can't do that unless You change my way of thinking)
—Edith Matthies

PREFACE

...this is openly a kind of spiritual autobiography,
But the trick is that on any other level
it's a kind of insane collage of fragments of memory.

–Jonathan Lethem

All memoirs are suspect...they are after all our personal memories. Anyone who has adult children realizes that childhood incidents are remembered differently by everyone involved. The variety of unique memories or perspectives of any given event is dependent only on the number of individuals present.

And so it is with the following thoughts. There will be many events others will remember differently and for those prospective eventualities, I ask for clemency in advance. My memories are fallible, my perception no doubt often skewed; I do not purport to have complete truth of what I remember. However, what is written below is, to the best of my ability, truth; at least from my viewpoint!

I write for my children and grandchildren, in order that they may understand the wealth of their heritage and to give them a more complete picture of their maternal grandparents. My father died unable to enjoy all but one of fourteen grandchildren. I write so they will understand their mother better. With a more complete understanding of their parent, my children may be inclined to forgive frustrations they may have had in their growing up years.

A new little one arrives in our arms, and when disciplining begins, we first bring our own childhood experiences to the table. Those experiences come with our own perspectives, memories and perceptions. Proportionately, we either imitate, or resist our parents' methodology. Rarely does one generation of parents fully recapture how they themselves were parented. This happens, I believe, for a number of reasons. Methods of disciplining children are often cyclical, often faddish. As parents we grow in wisdom and discard which things, in our opinion, are superfluous or counterproductive. Certainly we would never want it said of us that we are repeating the mistakes we perceived in our parents!

I was a mother who was continually searching for a wider, better understanding of the contemporary world around her. It seemed I was always looking for a lifestyle and belief system congruent with the implications of a life following Jesus. As well, I was constantly unwinding the intertwining of Godly truth and steeped Mennonite tradition. This meant a continual shedding of one and clothing with another. Clearly, only the future will determine how successful I was.

Come, Walk With Me

With Me

A Life Lived With Joy

"Commit your way
to the Lord;
trust also in Him
and He shall bring
it to pass."
Psalm 37:5

1

BEGINNINGS

*Now he who supplies seed to the sower and bread for food will also supply
and increase your store of seed and will enlarge the harvest of
your righteousness.*

2 Corinthians 9:10

The prairie fields of Southern Alberta in 1943 were desolate, windswept, and uninviting. Only the most determined, the very hardy, and those with mountain moving faith would have the inner fortitude to envision a promising future in the bleak of the Canadian prairie. Leonard and Anna Adrian, however, were just such people. The land given to them where farm life began was seen as a gift direct from the Hand of God. They envisioned a life of physically hard work from dawn until dusk, but also that their little cabin would be filled with warmth, serenity and security.

My father had always assumed he would not marry, but would remain single as the Apostle Paul. However, in 1935 he was persuaded that this was perhaps not the Lord's will for him and he asked Anna Baergen to marry him. The 'pick-up line' with which he approached his bride to be, "I feel the Lord is saying I should ask you to marry me" was indicative of his naivety, lack of sophistication and tendency toward literal interpretation of Scripture! No matter, the line worked and the young couple married in October of 1935 when my father was thirty-five years old, my mother thirty-two. Their first years of married life were spent in Wembly, Alberta where my father was a Bible School teacher. It was then they heard of land being available in Rosemary, Alberta. They would become those who were known as 'Homesteaders'; they were given land with the understanding that the land would be tilled to become productive and that homes would be established, thereby populating western Canada. They were also assured there were farmers in Rosemary who had preceded them; these farmers would generously allow the use of their farm machinery in helping erect a house for the young couple. The quarter section later proved to be less than optimally fertile, in fact, stubborn to the point of barrenness, the soil being blessed with a rich deposit of gumbo. My parents, however, came with much optimism. They began life in Rosemary in a tiny three room cabin without insulation to protect them from the harsh Canadian winter and only a cook stove for warmth.

It was into this setting that my brother Peter was born in 1938, Herman, in 1940, and David, in 1941. Brother Peter recounts the excitement of our father driving onto the yard in mid-afternoon the middle of April, 1943, and announcing to his three sons that they had a sister. Although such news needs to be taken with great deliberation and thought in terms of what the future dynamics will be in a home with three sons and youngest daughter, no such pondering occurred, I'm told. Everyone was delighted that a girl had arrived and life promised to be decidedly different, and of course it was!

2

MY FATHER

It is a wise father who knows his child.
But maybe it's a very wise child
who takes time to know his father.

—Anonymous

Leonard Adrian
(1900-1967)

My parents' geographic ancestry, across a number of generations, involved migrations from the Netherlands to Poland, and then to Russia. My father, Leonard Adrian, was born in the village of Spat, in Crimea, Russia. At age eleven his family moved to become land owners in Omsk, Siberia.

He was twenty-one, when he heard the Lord speak to him. I cannot remember if he heard an audible voice or if, in his spirit he heard the Lord asking him to emigrate from Russia. Soon thereafter, in 1926, he said goodbye to his widowed mother and turned his face toward Canada. Canadian Immigration records recorded his arrival in Halifax, Nova Scotia, with the princely sum of one hundred dollars in his possession. My father would be the only male member of his immediate family to survive Stalin's atrocities. Many years later he learned from his sister who had remained in Russia that even on her deathbed his mother had mourned my father's leaving. Although my grandmother had initially given her blessing to my father when he emigrated, she had never been able to come to terms with his decision.

My father, who was always 'Papa' to me, had bushy dark eyebrows, what we called a 'Roman' nose, and a generous mouth. He was probably only five feet seven inches tall with a bit of a slump in his shoulders. I remember often being encouraged to "sit up straight"; in later years I have heard from those who knew him that I have, in fact, inherited that bit of a slouched back.

As a young child, certainly before the age of twelve, my Dad and I spent a lot of time playing checkers and *Mensch Erger Dich Nicht* (The German version of "Sorry"). This happened most often during the quiet Christmas season when the snow was piled high outside and the wind whistled through the cracks around the heavily frosted window panes. Jack Frost decorated the inside of the window as well as the outside. The only winter tasks beckoning my Dad were the morning and evening chores; caring for the horses, cows, pigs, and chickens. Those were the times that we spent carefully adding up the weekly income from the sale of milk and cream as well as the income from harvesting the grain. My Dad was a man of deep integrity, so getting the annual sales figures ready for Revenue Canada was a very serious matter for him. Those were warm family times, both because of the brave little oil heater which would be hard at work in the small living room but also because of the warmth of affection between my three brothers, my Dad, my Mom, and me. Dad loved to use this time to tell Bible stories, but also to read to us from German children's story books. My favorites were the German fables.

These were also the times we heard about the 'old country.' In my memory bank, life in the former Russia was far superior to life in Canada; often we heard of the abundant harvests, and the amazing vegetables and fruits which the land produced. The hard working, obedient horses were showered with love; their recently brushed, black coats always gleamed, their stalls were pristine, their hay brought to them on time and in abundance. My Dad described lots of play time with his friends, and was very clear about the difficulty that faced him in school. He did not like school.

My Dad was an optimistic farmer. Hopefulness bubbled out of his early morning voice as he sang his way to the cow barn. He had the unique (but questionable) ability to sing a myriad of old hymns, all to the same tune! In the barn—the gentle snuffling of the cows, and the happy grunts of the pigs, all assured him that God was on his side. We often heard him pontificate "There's no life like that of a farmer." His rationale was "where else could you be your own boss, work as early or as late as you wanted, and be accountable only to yourself?" I would later privately speculate "Be your own boss? Really?" Control was certainly pulled out of the hands of the farmer when the hailstorms pelted down, flattening an entire promising crop in a matter of minutes, leaving only the devastation of what had been a hope-filled summer. Where was the farmer's control when the heavens belligerently withheld rain, when the frost came too early and only reluctantly pulled itself off fields just as summer was starting? However, no one could convince my father that there was a better profession than that of a landowner farmer

My Dad was a lay minister during all of my growing-up years. Our local Mennonite church administrative structure at the time was such that there were three or four lay ministers who would take turns preaching the Sunday morning sermon, with one

Bishop (*Altester*) overseeing the ministry. During my developmental years in Rosemary the Bishop was Rev. J. D. Nickel. The lay ministers were not salaried; they were volunteer pastors who earned their living as farmers.

My dad felt an enormous responsibility to share God's word with integrity and passion. Many times he 'preached' the upcoming sermon to our cows and pigs, the most sanctified animals in the neighborhood. His understanding of the call to discipleship was a hard and narrow road. He firmly believed we would one day be asked to give an account for the diligence with which we shared the gospel story. He felt huge trepidation whenever he would be preaching, not from a fear of public speaking but from the fear of possibly sharing his own thoughts, rather than those the Lord was giving him for that particular morning. This understanding of God's call, and his accountability to God, formed his approach to his ministry.

His sermons were consistently well thought out and organized; never boring. Regardless what Biblical reference text he chose for the morning's teaching, my father always inserted the salvation message. Papa's preaching was often likened to that of the biblical Jeremiah since invariably he would be overcome with emotion before his sermon ended. His sermons were never a collection of quotes from other teachers, nor were they book reports. In retrospect, because his messages did not soothe egos, his thoughts on a Sunday morning may have often been unpopular.

My father saw his ministry to the church as his first responsibility. While other young farmers may have spent their evenings strategizing ways to increase productivity, Papa would probably have been meditating on the Scripture God had highlighted to him that morning. Given that scenario, it could have been easy to assume he was perhaps not the most gifted farmer in Rosemary. I would challenge that line of thought. When he immigrated to

Canada at age twenty seven, my father left a substantial farm estate. At that age he would certainly have been, not only knowledgeable, but instrumental as well in the success of the family farm. It follows that he would have been well aware of wise farming practices. As well, my brothers more than I, remember Dad as being a master at improvisation—making do, adjusting in whatever manner he could to use strategies and materials he had on hand. Cash to buy new equipment was always in short supply. However, Papa found great joy in being able to be both a minister and a farmer. When the Lord gave him three sons he envisioned them sharing his love of farming but that future did not materialize.

Viewing my father from an adult perspective, I saw him as being miscast. Although he loved laughter, jokes, and telling stories or fables, his theology would not allow him to enjoy life in that dimension. Traditional Mennonite teaching would have ingrained in my father that hilarity, laughter that bubbled out uncontrollably, or quick-witted humor were incongruent with a serious walk of faith. A truly mature Christian was to be somber with an appreciation of the soberness of a life of 'suffering for Jesus.' Although, I believe my Dad instinctively knew that was wrong theology, others in his place of authority felt likewise. This role to which he was miscast had an important and troubling influence upon my position in my family and community.

My own enjoyment of humor was interpreted as an, from his childhood teaching, indication of my shallow faith. I seemed to absorb my father's thinking even though, in my head, I could easily discern the falseness in that conclusion. The requirement to suppress my delight in humor seemed incongruent with how I was created. However, these childhood assumptions have deep roots. I was well into adulthood before I was able to shed that diagnosis of my walk of faith, exchanging it for a life of joy.

As an aside, in Bible school the principal called me into his office so he could chastise me for what he saw as my shallow faith. He remarked, "What would your father say if he could see how you laugh here." I remember thinking, "You surely don't think it would be news to him?" Very rarely had I heard my Dad burst out into uncontrollable laughter; enough though I know it was a part of his DNA. When he spoke of my grandmother he would remark that she too enjoyed a good laugh. Over the years, some of my peers have shared their remembrance of Dad's spontaneous reaction with laughter. Since laughter has often defined my days, I cherish that inheritance from him!

I can still hear my Dad say to us children *"Ich bin Euch Allen so sehr Gut,"* (You are all so dear to me.). That was as close as he could come to saying "I really love all of you." It was sufficient; we certainly all knew the depth of his affection for us. I am reminded of the quote by Jean Paul Richter: "What a father says to his children is not heard by the world but it will be heard by posterity." Often in the mornings when farming was slow, and I was at a pre-school age, there would be time for me to crawl onto his lap after breakfast. He enjoyed a few minutes where he would tell Bible stories.

Although never abusive, my father was a strict disciplinarian. I believe that his understanding of corporal punishment was thrust on him as a child; he knew nothing different. He felt a great accountability for the morality and faith of his children. In his view, when we children failed, it became his failure.

Our father would not allow himself to enjoy our successes because, among Mennonites, pride was an anathema, an abomination. Theology dictated that God resisted the proud; therefore, our accomplishments as children were carefully unrecognized. It would not do to hear "you did a great job," or "you can be so proud of yourself" in the Adrian household. I don't remember this with any sourness or bitterness; our parents were adhering to what they believed were the Godly principles for child rearing. Regardless of how irrational or harsh the discipline seemed at the time, we children never doubted our parents' love for us. To be entirely fair, I do have to repeat a comment from my mother that Dad was hesitant to discipline me as diligently as my older brothers since I was a 'fragile girl.' Being female did have its small privileges.

After 26 years of farming, the Rosemary farm was sold in the winter of 1964 and my parents retired to Abbotsford, British Columbia. Dad continued to speak itinerantly in the West Abbotsford Mennonite Church until he became ill in the fall of 1966. He did not recover and died July 15, 1967.

I have thought, many times with sadness, that I never was able to develop an adult relationship with my father. I left Rosemary right after high school and never again lived near my father. The few short months, when married, that I lived in Vancouver and he lived in Abbotsford were not long enough to crawl out of our pre-existing relationship dynamics; the child/parent rut that was irrevocably entrenched after twenty-three years of re-enforcement. That lack of an adult-adult relationship with my father remains a loss not only for me but also for Ben, for our children and for our grandchildren.

Had he stayed with us longer, I believe he would have loved his grandchildren lavishly without the parental expectations that had lain so heavily on his shoulders during our growing up years. The suit of expected perfections from others, the unrealistic demands he foisted on himself, being misunderstood because of his passion for the Lord: all of this clothed him. It was ready to be shrugged off when he retired to BC. Given more days he could have been released into a new definition of himself.

In my view he had an unconscious desire to be free; free to encourage his children and their spouses. I would have cherished him filling my "father's blessing" bucket as he experienced a freedom from the glass house that had been placed around him in Rosemary.

Each of us is left to emulate our own interpretation of what Dad's possible lengthened life span would have looked like in our own lives. It is a truth; however, that as God takes our parents home, our Heavenly Father slides into the parental role. When the Creator Himself parents us, we were, and are, then in the best of all possible parental worlds.

3

MY MOTHER

*"My mother...she is beautiful, softened
at the edges and tempered
with a spine of steel.
I want to grow old and be like her."*

~ Jodi Picoult

Anna Baergen Adrian
(1903-2004)

My mother, Anna Baergen, was born in the steppes of southern Ukraine in the turmoil of July, 1903. She was the third child and also third daughter in a family of nine children born to Gerhard and Maria (Goerz) Baergen. A farmhand to her father, she shouldered the farming responsibilities when her father was conscripted into the Russian army. In her late teens at the time, she was responsible for the seeding of the crops that first year, but her father rescued her from that responsibility the next spring. Mama remembered the ominous cloud which covered her as she saw someone striding toward their farm in the distance. Then came the sunshine of great relief when she realized it was her father coming home from the conscription. It has been said that she was her father's favorite child, I assume partially at least because she was a willing and capable work-mate for him. Shortly thereafter the marauding Tartars destroyed their farm; confiscated their horses and the Baergens were left homeless.

Along with seven of her siblings, Mama arrived in Canada in 1924 at the age of twenty-one. Shortly thereafter Mama was hired as a 'kitchen girl' although she could not speak English. Her employer, with patient compassion taught her to speak and read English, her primer was a cookbook. She was painfully shy, self-effacing, but blessed with unusual insight and compassion into the human dilemma. Mama was beautiful with black hair and blue eyes, carrying herself straight and tall; reserved in her bearing and demeanor.

In my childhood and teenage years she was totally defined by her position as a minister's wife in a strong patriarchal society where women waited, often a lifetime, to be given credibility. My mother was no exception. She lived a life being continually subjected to judgmental public opinion. Her life on the farm was very difficult. She was the helper to my father, working side by side with him as they cared for cows, pigs, geese, horses, and chickens. When the children were little, her role demanded that she continue to work shoulder to shoulder with my father, doing whatever farm work needed to be done.

Mother had a fear of heights; my father considered this irrational, probably, because overcoming fear was such a necessity in farm life. Regardless of that fear, day after day, she was required to gingerly step across a flume (a fifty foot long and a twelve inch wide board walk, somewhat like a viaduct) spanning a narrow gorge filled with rushing water twenty five feet below. Beyond this 'death trap' the cows waited patiently for her to come relieve them of their milk. She would then determinedly push down her fear, *schlepping* the full milk buckets again over the culvert, and carrying them the half-mile home. The oldest child, Peter, at age six, was required to look after his three younger siblings during the milking process, which, I assume, would take her at least an hour. She remembered him following her to the field in total frustration because one of the younger ones would not stop crying and Peter, feeling very responsible, was afraid something was terribly wrong.

I remember my mother being very capable, but without the confidence to see herself with clarity. Often Mom would comment she was uncomfortable with her English diction when in fact; she had a very good command of the language. By nature stoic, in her later years my mother often seemed needled with regret; dragging a sense of failure with regard to her social skills, her parenting, and her personal walk of faith. In those arenas her determined cheerfulness was defeated. Perhaps it was the natural aging process that highlighted this sadness in her life.

Remembrance brings back my experiences of finding elaborate dress patterns and fabric from the Sears catalogue. I would then command a performance from my own private seamstress. Sewing for a demanding daughter was clearly not a delightful experience for my mother, visited on her prior to every Christmas season. She would graciously do her best; the festive dress invariably was sewn wonderfully on her Singer treadle machine.

In the years our sons were active in after-school activities, especially during soccer season, I recall how many times we would juggle dinnertime to accommodate their timetables. Such was never the case on the farm. Meals were served at the same time every day with no one missing. Although simple, meals were started early in the afternoon partly because convenience foods were convenient only to those who weren't saddled with the cooking and partly because of the undependability of the cook stove. I have often wondered how my mother managed to produce the delicious meals and heavenly baking in light of the very limited financial resources, no electricity, no refrigeration, and only one cookbook. The phrase "we Mennonites lived out of the flour sack" was often used to describe the majority of the ethnic Mennonite meals. Flour and sugar, in various forms such as syrup, or molasses seemed to be the one consistent staple in many homes, especially in Ukraine. This habit migrated to Canada with the Mennonite immigrants from Ukraine.

When the garden was smiling, offering up fresh radishes, kohlrabi (my personal favorite), succulent peas and sweet carrots, the dilemma of creating meals for a family of six became far less weighty; even somewhat of a pleasure. During the weeks when corn was harvested, our supper meal would often be just that—all you can eat of the corn cobs bulging with plump kernels smothered with butter and topped with salt. What a great treat that was. Sometimes Mom would add crisply fried potatoes or freshly salted cucumbers. Another favorite, but very labor intensive, meal was one of homemade noodles served with fried onions and gravy. Should there be any noodles left over, they too would be fried for another meal and topped with glistening, translucent onions. Nothing dominated the kitchen aroma like fried onions. These grew freely in the Alberta gumbo-like soil as did other root vegetables; carrots, potatoes, turnips and parsnips. In fall when the pig was butchered—or when, in later years, we would buy a side of beef, or kill the last of the chickens—Mom would preserve the meat that was not smoked by canning it. She was wonderfully proficient at canning meatballs, roast beef, and chicken. Opening up a jar of meatballs on a Sunday for lunch filled not only the need for physical sustenance but met an emotional need for security in the knowledge that we would have enough to eat for the winter. I learned to love headcheese, the mere mention of which causes my children to turn green.

It goes without saying that, throughout my growing up, my Mom invariably chose the martyr's path; the burnt toast was hers, the piece of chicken no one else would eat, or going without dessert if there wasn't enough to go around. That would be one of the good Mennonite 'mamma' traditions that didn't seem to want to be passed on to me!

I do remember some really lean years when, opening up my lunch bucket at school, I would find the center of my sandwiches filled not with peanut butter, jam or syrup but lard on which Mom had sprinkled some sugar. I guess it really was just another version of butter which the pig had sacrificed as opposed to the traditional contribution from the cows.

There were winter months when we weren't able to sell milk so dollars weren't available to buy coffee, then Mom and Dad would grind up wheat or even rye and call it 'Pripps.' We also had Postum which was a precursor to Instant Coffee. Postum would see us through until we could again buy the real thing. Wikipedia tells me Postum was a caffeine free, fat free, trans-fat free, sodium free and sugar free granulated drink made from wheat bran, wheat, molasses and malt dextrin from corn.[1] Created in 1895, it became immensely popular during the war years when coffee was rationed. Its production was discontinued as recently as 2007. Even as a little girl I remember sitting at the breakfast table with Mom sharing a cup of coffee, mine would be poured into a saucer so that it could cool quickly while I either dipped my toast or a roasted zwieback into it.

1   Postum, last edited on 5 June 2017, accessed August 03, 2017, https://en.wikipedia.org/wiki/Postum.

My mother, I believe, had a direct pipeline to the Almighty when determining what discipline style her only daughter needed. She never raised her voice at me that I can recall, but her few words of deep disappointment, or rebuke were enough to make me cringe. In retrospect, although my Mom used few words, I was in no doubt about her *Welt Anschaung,* her standard for behavior, her self-imposed conversational principles. Even in the years when she was over ninety she was able to speak into my life with such graciousness that I don't ever recall being offended by her opinion: frustrated, yes—because it tended to cramp my style at times.

Mom lived her 101 years in a world that she could not possibly understand. At one point, when I was trying to describe the function of the fax machine, I remember her telling me, "You could tell me you were being transported like the Biblical Philip and I would believe you. None of it makes any sense to me!" (Philip, whose story is outlined in Acts 8 verse 39, was transported by the Spirit of the Lord from one city to another in an instant). Social mores, the evolution, and explicitness of TV and the more graphic novels of our generation were all arenas she navigated as she tried to marry her faith with modern society. It left her quite unsure, but as I heard her pray, she always reverted back to what she knew best, thankfulness to her changeless Heavenly Father.

In the turmoil of the charismatic movement of the 1970's, I clearly remember a conversation we had. Mom challenged me (in German of course): "Are you telling me that in all these years of knowing my Heavenly Father I have not been filled with the Holy Spirit because I've not had a second experience?" That single, genuine, painful question from a woman who had authentically walked with God for over seventy years brought an adjustment to my perception of the charismatic movement. It has served as a plumb line for me whenever I hear of a 'new move of God' and it has reinforced my thankfulness for the foundational faith instruction given so intentionally by my parents.

My Mom's thirty-seven years as a widow were spent in Clearbrook, BC. Ben and I chose to move to Prince George just two months after my Dad passed away. Today, from my perspective of being ten years older than my mother was when she was widowed, I am appalled at my callousness. I was her only daughter and thought nothing of deserting her in that first year of grief. It is indeed hardest to forgive one's own mistakes. My Mom never reflected any sourness at our moving; she had the uncanny ability to release her children to go where and when we felt we needed to go. Her stance with her adult children has been a guideline that I have often felt compelled to copy, regardless of the personal difficulty it required of me.

Many times in the ensuing years, as we drove down to Clearbrook from Prince George, she would encourage us to begin the ten-hour drive back north earlier rather than later; never clinging to us even though it was clear our family would be missed. Mom would often remark that although she was alone, she never admitted to being lonely. Personally, knowing the relationship she demonstrated with her Heavenly Father, I believe she used frequent conversations with Him to cover the loss of my Dad. It was a deliberate choice she made to view life positively, refusing to be a victim.

Mom seemed to always be determined to take charge of her life and make it look the way she wanted to. Because of this mind set, it was difficult for her to ask for a 'ride' to church on Sunday mornings but she persevered and did just that for many years. Being dependent on others was very hard for her. As long as she was able, she would walk the half dozen blocks to the grocery store, reluctant to use a walker until it became impossible for her to navigate without that support.

She left her peaceful home on Fir Street in Clearbrook, BC. to move to a two bedroom condominium a block away. She furnished it modestly; often espousing the theory that life was so rich for her that she couldn't justify new furniture. The local Mennonite Central Committee used furniture store was her favorite haunt. The condominium had two bedrooms which meant that when our family took up residence in the summer or over Christmas, our long legged teenagers would lay like loaves of bread tucked beside each other on the living room floor. The only time they minded this 'hotel' was in the summer weeks when I would insist on taking them to Clearbrook to do their part in removing the plump raspberries from their thorny bushes. I coerced them out of bed at 5:30 in the morning; slipped plastic bags over their feet to ward off the heavy dew. Then I would prop them up beside the empty raspberry flats and cajole them into going to work, enticing them with ideas of how their lucrative pay cheques could be spent. Clearly this was not their idea of how to spend time at Oma's house, although it didn't diminish their affection for her.

From there my Mom moved into a condominium in the Independent Living Complex at the Menno Home in Abbotsford, BC, then to the Menno Home, and lastly to the Menno Hospital. Each move was met, not with bitterness, but with compliant resignation. She was able to maintain her pleasant demeanor until she went to her heavenly home, so much so, the staff at the hospital remarked often on her cheerfulness. As children we were able to give our tributes to her on her 95th birthday party. My thoughts on the depth of her mentorship in my life as I saw it at my age of 55 are delineated in the following chapter. She was, without a doubt, the most influential woman in my life. Her legacy is certainly one to which I aspire.

Her last public birthday in the Menno Hospital was at age one hundred when she was barely able to speak but was still mentally, fully alert. She remains the portrait of a life well lived; gracious, kind, with immovable internal strength and a faith deeply rooted in God. I trust that her genes have fully been transplanted within me.

Additional insight into the life of my mother may come with the reading of *Anna's Story* which I wrote as a tribute to the life of my mother.

4

FOR MY MOTHER AT 95
July 29, 1998

I have always known that the most important teaching you
wanted to drill into my head, Mom,
was that I would know the ways of God and
that you needed to teach me about the character of God.
Over and over I heard you tell me about the faithfulness of God.
As a child you told me He was my loving heavenly Father and
That, for all my failings, His mercy is new every morning.
When I was frustrated with the flies, the chicks, the spiders,
the pigs, you taught me that He is the Father to all He has made;
that all of creation is waiting for the new Heaven and the new Earth.

When I left home you told me that His strength was available
to me in whatever situation I found myself.
Leaving for Mississippi, you assured me that He would never leave me,
but would walk closely beside me; and truly,
He never fell asleep looking after me.

When you taught me about homemaking,
you talked to me about God being a God of order.
When I got my first job, from you I learned that whatever role
I was given in life, the goal was to do everything as if I were doing it,
or playing the role, for my Heavenly father.
We talked of my being a wife, and well, you did your very best to teach
me about
submission in the way you saw was God honoring!
I learned from you that God was able to infuse me
with patience for being a mother to my three sons,
and that my Heavenly Father loved my children even more than I did;
they were only lent to me for a time.

You taught me about relationships according to Proverbs:
Without gossip, a quarrel dies down;
A gentle answer turns away anger.
A trustworthy person keeps a secret.
He who covers an offence rather than exposing it,
Promotes love

I have often reflected on the fact that,
until I was seventeen, I thought all Mennonites were perfect;
the negative personality traits of others were
not discussed within my hearing during my childhood,
(either that or I just didn't perceive it).
I watched you walk through difficult years on the farm,
always with the attitude,
"the Lord knows and His way is the best way."
Most of all you showed me that
the fear of the Lord is the beginning of all wisdom.

We all want to leave a legacy of achievements,
changes for good we've initiated or things we've accomplished.
For you, I know that it's most important that your Heavenly Father
will one day say to you "well done, good and faithful servant"
but today, on this earth, from those who know you best
and have come behind you, we say we have found you faithful.

5

EULOGY FOR MY MOTHER
July 29, 1903 – October 27, 2004

Our Mother passed through the intercourse of daily life
with the delicate tact that never inflicts pain.
Shy and self-diminishing,
she determined to adapt to any situation with equanimity
mit gelassenheit and strength from her Heavenly Father.
She knew her Lord for nearly a century and I believe not a single day
did she fail to have an audience with the King.
She embodied Proverbs 31:
"Beauty is fleeting, charm is deceptive,
but the woman who fears the Lord is to be praised."
She loved her children and grandchildren unconditionally
and individually prayed for each one tirelessly.
Was she faultless?
Of course not, she just had so many good qualities,
it's very easy to forget the few faults!
Intellectually, we know she is where she has longed to be;
restored and at rest,
still, in our hearts and in our lives,
we feel the loss of someone who is irreplaceable.

-Edith

6

TO SAY GOODBYE

She lies, eyes closed, breathing slight,
feathered, wisps of white hair caressing the pillow.
I gently kiss her forehead; she stirs.
Mother, when did you no longer need me?
You have distanced yourself from me,
each visit brings a new crush of loss
somewhere in this, the last year of your life,
you have removed yourself from me.

Is it a preparing for the beyond?
Those invisible walls blocking my affection?
I have driven long hours,
solely to sit by your bedside,
watching your shallow breath disappear in and out.
You cannot speak. I understand;
I accept one-sided conversation,

I know you hear, surely you still perceive.
You always had intuitive knowing,
even in a world so foreign to your comfort.
My gentle Mother, I don't ask for your solace,
does my being here meet no need in you?
Sadness and pain stir as I see you drifting away.
Let me be enough for you, just for now.
I sense such withdrawal.

Have we not been friends for years?
Adversaries at fifteen are surely friends at sixty.
What hidden frustrations trouble you, my dear Mother,
as you lay unmoving in your bed?
I beg to reverse roles; allow the daughter to soothe, to comfort.

Countless times we spoke of your imagined inadequacies,
your falsely remembered failures,
the lies that attack your essence.
I have reached into the beyond, grasping words to
bring a new view of yourself...
have you only heard more failure?

Let me in!! Let me show you adequacy,
demonstrate reliability
I can speak comfort, courage, and understanding.
How can I convince you?
Is it so difficult to allow me into your hidden world
and share this final passage?
And so I sit quietly, hour upon hour, reminiscing.
Yearning, holding tightly to the cord that threads
between us, yet needing to set you free.

Then, it's time, yet another good-bye;
how many times have I said a final farewell?
"May the Lord bless you and keep you.
May He make His face to shine upon you,
And be gracious unto you.
May the Lord turn his face toward you,
and give you His Peace."
Whispering, "maybe next time will be in another world,"
I slip away yet again.

Imminent the news of your drifting away
from your body and from me.
In that finality I will grieve for what could have been
in this, the last year of your life.

But, I will not, I will choose to celebrate
who you were to me for all my sixty years.
This will be my catharsis, my cleansing.
And to future wanderings into the past
where fondly cherished remembrances of you still live...
I will embrace them all...with thanks.

                                    -February 14, 2004

"Where'd the days go, did was play? When all we that we were under And the stress stress at all, just wasn't and a jump into a run fall." a harmless —Paolo Nutini

7

CHILDHOOD

Rosemary, Alberta, in 1943, a town of a few hundred residents plus several hundred more from its outlying farms, proudly claimed a small hospital. It is indicative of the changing landscape of Canadian healthcare that we were able to sustain not only a country doctor, but also a fully-staffed hospital.

On April thirteenth 1943, the obstetrics ward was unusually busy, so much so, that in a twenty-four hour period, two male and one female baby were born. Rudy Dyck, Ed Wiebe and I all entered the world within a twenty-four hour period. We grew up together, moved to various parts of the country, married, and now, having walked through all the obligatory successes and failures of life, have come to enjoy one another's company very much by email and in person. Together with our spouses, as well as with our dear friends, Lee and Leona (Penner) Bajer, we began celebrating our birthdays together in 2005, when we officially became senior citizens.

Following this prolific day in the Rosemary hospital obstetrics department, I grew up as one of those fortunate few who have had a happy and basically uneventful childhood. In my pre-teen years the hardships of farm life without running water (and therefore no inside plumbing); telephone, or electricity, slid effortlessly over me. I knew nothing different, and life was just what it was. My three older brothers were delighted to have a sister; as a result I became the favorite and was probably cocooned from the harshness of our poverty. In 1948, with four growing children and two adults living in a small three room 'cabin,' our father decided to extend the cabin and it became, while not large, certainly in my view, quite adequate.

There were two bedrooms downstairs, and one large bedroom upstairs that housed my three brothers, and there was an unfinished attic which was used as a storage room. I remember the wonderful smell of freshly smoked farmer's sausage coils being hung from the rafters in the attic. In fall, the mouthwatering fragrance would permeate the whole house. My brothers were given the 'upper room' where my dad built a small closet and then found a double metal bedframe as well as a single one. Initially our mattresses were large duvet sacks filled with straw; prickly at first, but they soon softened as we bounced around.

'A simple dish from the loving hand of my mother nourished and replenished both body, and soul.'

We had a nice sized farm kitchen where the gush, the trickle, and the explosions of air coming out of the water pump seemed to be synonymous with the turbulent pattern of farm life. Sometimes life on the farm was serene and smooth as a window pane, other days it seemed anything that could go wrong did; anything that could break, did break; and every frustration that could visit us, darkened our door. That was the 'dailyness' of family life on the farm. Off the kitchen was a small washroom. This housed a shiny red hand water pump and the gray, aluminum dipper, handy for all to grab a drink or dip some water into the wash up basin. We never worried about passing on germs. The white enamel basin with its red rim was always in place ready to catch the water dripping from the pump or for the required hand and face washing before every meal.

My mother would make her own soap with a mixture of lye crystals, water and lard. Even today some artisans enjoy soap-making using the same three components, water, sodium hydroxide, and lard. Contrary to the images which come to mind when one thinks of those ingredients, the soap was actually not harsh but very gentle. Baths were taken once a week, on Saturday nights. I have come to understand this was a common practice in homes without running water. The youngest bathed first, the oldest last, all in the same tub of water. Our tub, for some odd reason, was shaped like a fishing boat; one end square; the other sloped upwards. It was positioned in the small washroom and we were all treated to the same bathwater. I remember a bed sheet partitioned the bathing from the rest of the kitchen. The outhouse was our only place of privacy for my first seventeen years.

'Washing, ironing and cleaning; baking, preserving, and canning.'

Next to the kitchen was an alley pantry. In my mind's eye I can still see the five-foot long shelves fastened to the left wall. At the end of the little alley was a small table on which rested a shiny aluminum cream separator. Twice daily the buckets of milk from the cows were swirled through this machine, separating the cream from the milk. These were then poured into cans and maneuvered outside where they were picked up by the truck taking them to be sold. This was our only income in the winter seasons. Since we didn't have a refrigerator, all our prepared foods, the annual box of apples, and Christmas candies as well as bags of flour, were all neatly stacked on shelves or on the floor. A freshly made Napoleon torte, three dozen oatmeal cookies, Saturday's fluffy *Zweibach*, or fragrant loaves of bread were all tucked on the shelves and covered with tea towels. In later years, when I was around thirteen years old, the convenience of the occasional plastic bag would make its way into our kitchen and was used to prevent Mom's baking from drying out. In our home bologna was an extraordinary treat. When it was brought home from the grocery store, sliced, and tantalizingly wrapped in brown paper, the temptation to sneak a slice proved too much for me. My life of crime had its genesis in that little pantry but I would find myself confessing my sin before the day was out. Truly, bologna is not the delicacy that I remember it to be seventy years ago.

Tucked in the corner of the pantry was the trapdoor to the cellar. The door in the floor was heavy, and when I managed to pull it up; force it to "stand up straight," the four steps yawned down into the earthen room below. From my earliest memories the cellar was foreboding; it was literally just a large hole in the ground covered with a house. It was dark, the smell of dampness was always in the air; the flashlight I used was dismally inadequate. The dim light cast shadows which only made the room more sinister and claustrophobic. In the middle of the small room was one wide row of shelving on which Mom would stack her jars of fruit preserves. On the floor in front of, and underneath the shelving were two large stone crock pots. In one Mom would make sauerkraut. That crock was stuffed with cabbage, only salt, vinegar and water were added. Mom would then use an old sledge hammer and a round piece of wood as a weight. The lid for the crock jar had disappeared. The other crock would be filled with cucumbers that would become dill pickles; the dill stalks were always swimming on top underneath a wooden lid. The unfinished ceiling of the 'cellar' was covered with solid two-by-four boards. The ceiling didn't quite meet the dirt walls, leaving a space of about eighteen inches. This was where Mom stacked her empty jars, as well as beet pickles, watermelon pickles or vegetable preserves. It became my daily chore to bring any of these creations upstairs to the kitchen. Along with these jars of canning the cellar was home to mice and salamanders of every description, common to all farm houses. Dust in gray lacy layers covered the dirt walls but still the dampness managed to glisten through. I dreaded going down to the cellar, so overcoming my fear was a daily exercise. Away from the house entirely, my Dad designed a root cellar which was really just a large hole in the ground covered with wooden slates designed to form a roof. Each year, before the ice left the farm pond, Dad would cut large chunks of ice. These were then covered with straw and tucked into the root cellar. The straw formed a barrier from the heat of the summer, during those hot months the root cellar kept all manner of fruit and vegetables cool.

In the fall Dad would order the heating coal for the winter's use. We would hear a truck arrive in front of the kitchen and a load of shiny black coal chunks was dumped in front of (as I remember it) an eighteen inch hole, which led into the cellar. We children threw the coal down into the cellar and from there we would bring it upstairs to the kitchen oven. In my early childhood years, this oven heated the entire 600 square foot house. The grate above the oven seemed to grab the heat sucking it upstairs to 'the boys' room' as we called it. In the bitter cold Alberta winter the only warm place downstairs was the four-foot area in front of the oven. I have fond memories of three of us children sitting on the heavy, open oven door keeping our rounded backs toasting. Since there were four children, I remember many good natured shoving matches where someone landed on the floor when their optimism about the width of the door exceeded reality.

Heating with coal meant a layer of black soot covered the kitchen wall, which was painted a light green. I remember washing the wall and being amazed at the clear, placid color smiling out at me after the spring-cleaning. It was probably the only cleaning session I found productive, which is why I remember it almost six decades later.

On the side of the oven was a large water reservoir. This six gallon container would be refilled every morning. The oven kept the water warm all day so it was ready to be used to wash dirty little faces as well as dishes. On Mondays, laundry day, the reservoir would be drained very quickly in order to fill the large washing machine. As a young child, I watched my mother diligently grind my brothers' jeans up and down, up and down, as I listened to the swoosh of the water as she bent over the glass-ribbed washboard. Then came the day we became the proud owners of a washing machine. Unfortunately, along with the convenience of the automatic agitation of the clothes, came a very loud, mentally abrasive motor with the overwhelming smell of oil and gas. No conversation could be carried on in the vicinity of this green intruder. Although it certainly made the physical effort of washing much less weighty, the loud grinding of the motor was mentally and emotionally debilitating. When Mom was finally able to shut it off at the end of the day, her energy was depleted as much by the constant roar as by the actual work of cleaning clothes. Washing jeans and heavy farm clothes in the winter time was most challenging. Mom would hang the jeans out to dry on the frozen wash line, bring them inside in the evening, frozen into mannequin likeness, and hang them upstairs in the attic to dry. The whole procedure from start to finish always took a few days in the minus forty degree weather.

Saturday, on the farm, was the day the house needed to be cleaned from top to bottom, everything dusted, and the linoleum floors washed It was *Zweibach* baking day, car washing day, shoe polishing day, ironing day...all those white shirts for four males had to be ready for Sunday 'go to meetin.'

For years I have been able to use the undependable, unpredictable heat of the farm stove and the lack of a proper thermometer on it as the reason for my lack of skill in the kitchen as a young bride. I believe my Mother despaired of her daughter ever becoming a proficient homemaker. She was able to manage that oven well, turning out cakes, cookies, butter horns, and other delectable baking with enviable expertise.... I was not.

'Dear music, I thank you for feeding my soul'

A serendipitous lifelong joy, has knit itself into my soul as a result of Saturday chores; it is the 'emotional massage' that is mine whenever I listen to classical music. As a pre-teen I was regularly sent upstairs to dust and clean my brothers' room. My first task was to find my brother Peter's record player and pop on one of his 'Light Classical' records. The process of procrastinating, thereby drawing out the dusting and cleaning, allowed me to fall in love with the music. And it has never changed: classical music continues to be my 'default.' In grade ten our youth group traveled the 160 km to Calgary to hear the Calgary Philharmonic Orchestra and Choir perform Handel's Messiah in the Calgary Jubilee Auditorium. As a young fifteen-year-old I thought I would never again reach the height of glitz, drama and magic I experienced in 1959. Remembering—nostalgia—brings back those feelings even today.

My love of music was energized when I was in the seventh grade. Lydia Braul, four years older than I, lived perhaps half a kilometer away from my home. She was the proud owner of a pump organ, not all of the keys were functional, but nevertheless, as far as I was concerned it was absolutely wonderful. The fact that Lydia could play this organ filled me with longing. She patiently showed me the basic two octaves on this old, much-loved organ. She was no longer interested in playing this instrument; she had a boyfriend! I capitalized on her new interest asking her if my Dad could buy the organ from them. I began to eat, sleep and dream of learning to play music. To set the stage for the plan of convincing my Dad to make this purchase, I promised him I would learn to play whatever hymn he desired. Finally the day came. Dad paid $25.00 for the organ, quite a princely sum in those days. I don't remember how the organ was transported from their home to ours, perhaps on the back of a wagon. It might have even been carried the short distance. It was dragged into my bedroom and I diligently I pounded away at the first two stanzas of "Jesus Loves Me." My brothers began to plan how they could throw me into a well, repeating the trick Joseph's brothers played on him. Eventually I graduated from only knowing one song and taught myself to play many, many of the old familiar hymns; often they're even quite recognizable

On Saturdays, when I would finish upstairs I would begin a 'tug of wills' with Mom. The tension centered around our little red RCA Victor radio. On Saturday afternoons, CFCN radio station out of Calgary streamed Western music, and I loved Kitty Wells, Hank Snow, Sons of the Pioneers, Gene Autry and other stars from that era. Mom, on the other hand, 'not so much! She felt the 'honkey tonk' message didn't contribute to the standards of morality she had in mind for me. Occasionally I would hear the beginnings of Kitty Wells' "*On the Wings of a Snow White Dove*," and would dive to crank up the volume to prove to my mother the spiritual value of western music.

'How many miles has this water travelled searching for our farm?'

In spring Dad would ceremoniously announce "time to clean the cistern," we would all troop out to the back of the house where, after saying, "now Edith stand back," he would grab the metal 'pull' on a round cement lid about four feet in diameter and open up the cistern. Our yearly water supply was housed in this round cement structure in the ground about twelve feet in diameter. The water would drain down the muddy irrigation canals from the Bassano Dam thirty miles away; then it would wander through the pastures, where cows, chickens, pigs and all other forms of living creatures would make use of the water before it trickled down to the Adrian farm. Once there, the water passed through a series of gravel strainers Dad had created to function as a filtering system.

Before we could add new water, the old water had to be cleaned out. Someone had to go down inside and scoop out the buckets of old water, invariably finding it had been home to a snake or a frog for the past months. Once the cistern had been mopped out, fresh/new water could begin to drain down in. During the first days after the cistern had been refilled, the pump inside the house would gush out the most unappealing, muddy water. However, after everything had settled and the new marine life had become comfortable, the water became quite clear, although it was extremely hard water with a lot of iron in it. I understand that some of the farmers would generously pour bleach into their cisterns; I don't remember that being our habit. Although we neglected the disinfectant, none of us ever contracted anything deadly from drinking the cistern water.

Our neighbors had an artesian well in their yard, quite close to the road. The well was considered community property, so often on a Saturday I would saunter to their yard with a couple of large buckets bringing home the soft, clear well water. If we should run out of water from our cistern, I remember Dad putting a barrel on an old 'stone boat' (a platform sitting on a couple of logs so it would slide behind a team of horses) and returning time after time to the artisan well to replenish our water supply. My memory could be inaccurate about the water being community property. In any case our neighbors, the Penner family and the Braul family, were very gracious in allowing us to use their water.

'Chaffing against the Mennonite definition of humility, modesty and decorum'

My father's opinion regarding women regulated most aspects of my life. During the summer before beginning grade five, I had the audacity to ask a lovely neighbor to be my hair dresser and cut off my braids. Unfortunately, Dad was very offended with my new look. Long braided hair was, what he considered to be, my crowning glory. He mandated that I stay home from church for three weeks so as not to bring shame on his parenting.

In grade six I yearned to play softball on the school team. This was certainly not a feminine activity from his perspective. In his German vernacular my father announced, "Not on my best day will my daughter play softball." It took a personal visit from my teacher before he would give his consent to my being on the soft-ball team; after all, it necessitated my cavorting with the ungodly 'English.' Because we lived six miles out of town, and the last bus left the school grounds at 4:30 pm, I would need to catch a ride to come home late from school. That, by itself, caused my Dad a great deal of trepidation.

In grade eleven, I took courage in hand when I sewed a sleeve-less blouse, and indeed, it was very hard for my father to allow his daughter to be seen in such risqué dress. We were to be seen as unassuming, humble, modest, and self-effacing. Many of the dogmatic decisions which he made were, I believe, because my father had an unending list of qualifications with respect to 'minister's children.' He had absorbed these as by osmosis from the most puritanical, the most rigid, or the most pious of those he was trying to emulate. Living in the fishbowl of Rosemary Mennonite society was challenging for both Dad and Mom.

When, in grade twelve, the news came to him that I was wearing shorts to play basketball at school, my sports career ended abruptly. I'm glad I never found out which saint felt compelled to educate my father about my burgeoning extra-curricular activities. I would probably still resent her and would be forced to forgive her, even at this late date. Facial makeup of any description was out of the question; a necklace was stretching the bounds of humility; certainly earrings were only for the 'English heathens.' Girls wearing 'men's pants' was an abomination. Amazingly, I swung my Dad over in my high school years and so was able to enjoy the GWG jeans that were so popular.

'No trinket, no toy, but love and security in gift wrap.'

Christmas and birthday celebrations, as I now reflect on the matter, were probably an incredibly stressful time for my mother. There was certainly never quite enough cash in December or on birthdays to satisfy even the most modest requests from the children for presents. It was for this reason I don't remember ever seeing my parents exchange gifts; which was certainly not because there was a lack of affection between my parents.

Our gifts were always ordered from the Simpson Sears catalogue. The omnipotent shipping clerks in the catalogue office felt free to substitute whatever they liked if the ordered item was no longer available. Often the gift that appeared on Christmas morning only slightly resembled the request, and was an enormous disappointment to us children. At the time I certainly never comprehended the frustration my mother must have felt as she anticipated our Christmas morning response. One year I had my heart set on a dresser set that included a hand held mirror, a comb, and a hairbrush, each with an ornate silver-colored handle. The substituted gift was a plain pink two-sided mirror. I am not proud of feeling obliged to brag to my friends about the magnificent dresser set that was now sitting on my dresser; but only in my imagination. Because my Heavenly Father is one who sees our deepest longings, He never forgot the unfulfilled yearning in that little girl's heart. When Christmas, 1966 came around, blinking at me from under the tree was a beautiful ornate silver three piece dresser set, courtesy of my soon-to-be husband. It was 'serendipity' from my Father's hand, letting me know that He had my emotional needs covered.

'There were long necked geese, snouted pigs, graceful horses, agile cats, loving dogs, clucking chickens and long suffering cows.'

Much of the labor-intensive side of our small mixed farm revolved around the animals we had. In the early spring Dad would come home from town with a load of chickens, maybe fifty or so. Being vulnerable to chills the chicks couldn't survive in the chicken coop for a time. Mom would find some cardboard to cover the floor and to fashion some walls to create a chick pen. These little chicks would squeak and peep in our kitchen, filling it with their distinctive new born fragrance. The chicks would stay in the kitchen until the weather warmed up enough so they could be moved into the chicken coop; a small building about twelve feet by twelve feet. Inside the chicken coop Dad built a shelf-like ledge and filled it with straw. Quickly the chicks would nestle in the straw and eventually lay their eggs. During the day the chickens would happily peck around on the yard finding worms and bugs. They always managed to slip into the coop through the swinging door when darkness closed in. The door was large enough for the chickens, but too small for the ever watchful coyotes looking to sneak a free meal. When electricity came to the farm, the newly hatched chicks would snuggle under a heat lamp in the coop for a week or so. The sacrificial chickens served up our daily ration of eggs and eventually graced our dinner table.

We usually had, as I remember it, two or so litters of pigs in the barn. They were pretty carefree, often they could be outdoors within a fence where they would dig and roll in whatever mud they could find. One or two pigs were butchered annually and the rest were shipped away. One year we had geese, but they terrorized me as a little girl, so they weren't allowed to call our farm home again.

Our herd of cattle--steers, cows, and one or two bulls—usually numbered close to one hundred. The cows, usually six or seven, provided milk, cream and butter, but needed to be fed morning and evening as well as taken out to the pasture in the morning and brought back for the evening. The cows became quite accustomed to hearing a call or whistle. Because the prairie fields are often barren, the lead cow could be seen raising her head when she heard the call from far away, and would begin to lumber home with her udder full of milk where she knew she would be relieved. The other cows would fall into a single line and all would wander home. If there were ditches to cross, or fences to limit their travel, I would bring them home on the road. One of the beef cows, usually a steer, was butchered in fall.

Every self-respecting farmer in Rosemary set aside one day in fall to bring home his cattle from the Lease Land. Lease Land was designated grazing pasture and was meant for the common use of all those in the community who needed it for their herd of cattle. Girls were never allowed to go out to the Lease Land. It was strictly a male domain; my Dad and his three sons enjoyed these fall events for the most part. I do remember one fall, however, when the number of cattle coming back home to the farm didn't jive with what my father expected. I remember Peter having to explain in great detail how he had unsuccessfully scoured the prairie looking for the errant calf. The next spring all our cattle were branded with our 'A4' brand before they were herded to the Lease Land. Branding ensured that they would not be taken home by another farmer in the fall. As I recall it was debatable who was more frustrated, Dad, because the calf was gone, or Peter who seemed unable to convince Dad that he truly had been very deliberate in his search and the calf was nowhere to be found.

Occasionally we had a bull as well. I heard the following story only in later years. It was the one altercation that we had with a neighbor who fancied himself a very wealthy rancher with cattle of enviable pedigree. He was pasturing his cattle just across the road from our farm. Among his cattle were some very delightful bovines, or so our bull thought as he was resting comfortably on our yard. He decided to go check out the neighboring scene; needing to explore his one area of expertise. Apparently he did so with great success. Unfortunately, our neighbor was most perturbed at the thought that his cows would bear a Hereford rather than an Angus calf sired by an overly friendly neighborhood bull. The result of the whole affair was that our neighbor took great umbrage; deciding to end the life of the bull. He did so in a most gruesome manner reminiscent of the scriptural encouragement, "if thine hand offend thee cut it off." Unfortunately the bull bled to death. I don't think my Dad was ever able to afford another one.

Farm life for the youngest child, and the only girl, was so very different from that of my older brothers. Were they to recall their stories, it would indeed seem that we had not grown up in the

same family. I loved 'being' outdoors, as opposed to working outdoors with my brothers, or being of actual substantial help with
farm work. I would do the mundane task of bringing the cows
home from the field, feeding the pigs, or teaching the young calves
to drink milk from a bucket, but I never really became proficient
at milking. While I was diligently working away at getting the
milk from Rosie, she was looking longingly over to where my
Mom would be milking with great skill.

*'It's fall, it's yellow grain, it's burning stubble, it's bright red
tomatoes, and oh my, it's smoked farmers sausages.'*

I do remember doing the stooking with my brother David.
Wikipedia tells me that a stook, is also referred to as a shock or
stack. It's is an arrangement of sheaves of cut grain stooks placed
so as to keep the grain heads off the ground while still in the field
and prior collection for threshing. The sheaves of grain were much
lighter than the heavy hay bales. I actually got the hang of standing the sheaves together into a little teepee-like. arrangement.
Five bundled sheaves to a stook, as I remember it. The threshing
machine would come as soon as possible and gobble up the stooks.
Threshing days were a time of high excitement for me in the early
years because we would have a couple of men come help get the
crop harvested. My mom would be busy cooking unusually wonderfully tasty meals in vast quantities, giving strict instructions
to us children that we were not welcome at the table until the
threshing crew had eaten.

The other annual event common to every Mennonite family
was the pig butchering. As I remember it, we would share the day
with at least two other families, and exchange the favor. When the
day ended we would have Mennonite farmer sausage and hams
smoking overnight. Dad built a smoking system whereby he could

hang the hams and sausages in a wooden wagon so they could swing freely, balanced on a piece of wood between the two sides of the wagon. The hams were then salted and hung in the garage (a misnomer really since I don't ever recall any vehicles being resident in the 'garage'). The pork hocks, heart, and tongue were cooked and pickled: liver sausage was a must. For me the crème de le crème meats were the crackles and ribs which cooked in a huge vat for hours and hours. The sausage casings were actual pig intestines cleaned and disinfected with brine. Considering today's paranoia (and it may be a well-deserved obsession) surrounding the dangers of food poisoning this does give one pause! Later the smoked sausages, spiced only with salt and pepper, were hung tantalizingly in our attic upstairs attic, the fragrance wafting down to the family kitchen.

School memories are few. Although I didn't particularly enjoy school, neither is it a really negative memory. I think I just felt that it had 'come to pass.' School did become far more interesting after grade ten. I became involved in electives like the Student Council and the Yearbook Committee. Those were also the years that we were all were getting our driver's licenses. School lunch hours meant riding in someone's car, sharing girlish secrets, checking out the opposite sex, and learning how to seductively swish our hair back and forth. I remember the thrill of getting my driver's license the day I turned sixteen and the cloak of maturity which (I assumed) surely was mine from then on.

Weekends were, by far the high points of the weeks. Saturday night was invariably choir night, which I loved. Our whole social life revolved around church events. Movies were out of the question; dances were held only in the Mormon Church, so not even in our orbit. Often the Sunday nights were designated as *Jugend Abend*, translated as a church service where the youth in the congregation were given the opportunity to plan and execute the evening gathering. Singing, a short devotional, a poem, and other such inspirational components were on the schedule. Sometimes these involved only the Sunday evening church service but more often it would include a bit of a social. Whether it was a funeral, or a wedding, a song festival or an anniversary celebration, the whole church body was invited. Not only were church activities our entertainment, and our spiritual school; they were the training ground and modeling on how to live life.

All of us growing up in Rosemary in the nineteen fifties, and probably the sixties, remember picking potatoes for the Japanese farmers in the fall. Proudly we brought home the massive amount of cash, $7.50 a day. It was hard work. In September the fields were full of young people hunched over, or crawling on hands and knees along the rows of dug up potato plants as their backs cried out for relief. We slowly made our way along the rows of potatoes, dragging a sack of harvested potatoes along behind us. When I was in grade eight the farmer that I worked for had invested in a potato picker so, from then on, we stood on the sides of the picker watching the belt belching up endless piles of potatoes and granite like clumps of dirt. It was my job to pull out the dirt so the cleaned potatoes could slide down into the sacks waiting at the back of the picker. We waited with expectation for morning and afternoon coffee break. Mornings…just coffee, but the afternoon break brought wonderfully soft sandwiches and hot sweet tea with milk. Often, before the crop was harvested, the first signs of winter blew across the fields, and we would find ourselves shaking, chilled to the bone. I remember asking the fellow who was driving the tractor if his cigarettes warmed his insides…it was tempting to try one just as an experiment.

The dollars at the end of a couple of weeks of picking came with the promise of winter clothes. These clothes were ordered from the Sears catalogue after hours of pouring over the pages, mentally matching sweaters to skirts, and jackets to jeans. One particular schoolteacher found the habit of his students arriving two weeks late to school very frustrating; it was a challenge for him to be professional to us—and so he was not. It became his habit to launch a few nasty, diminishing, well-timed, and well-directed comments which slipped out unchallenged. The targeted student was left humiliated exactly as the teacher intended. As a result, I always returned to school after potato picking season with a great deal of apprehension.

'Mortar boards in the air, the finish line, goodbye Rosemary High School'

High school graduation came in 1961. Our small high school gave us no options of course streams, and everyone who wanted to graduate had to do so strictly on academic merit. None of the trades which are so worthwhile in today's education system were available. In those years anyone wanting to be an electrician, plumber, or carpenter, for example, would not have found a great deal of the high school education to be of much value. 'Shop' and 'Home Economics' were the only options for electives. Our graduating class had been whittled down to seven of us who had passed the provincial exams. Rosemary society basically consisted of people from the Church of Latter Day saints, Mennonites and about a half dozen Japanese families. We Mennonites held ourselves quite separate from the Mormon people and vice versa. As a result we had a graduation ceremony in school but, a class dinner or prom were not a part of our celebration. It was an overwhelming fear for all of our parents that one or more of their children would select a life partner from the other faith. My parents left no doubt in my mind that socializing of any kind with Mormon boys was out of the question, but my-oh-my, they were just so handsome.

One memorable story must be submitted here since, in retrospect, it is indicative of our simple, unsophisticated pattern of growing up. It was 1960, October 31. My girlfriend Mary and I, along with two young men, were wandering the back roads of Rosemary, in search of something productive to do on Halloween Night. It had been an early fall, the ground was quite frozen and the temperature was well below zero. We were at the farm next to Mary's home. I decided it was an opportune time to use the outhouse; the cold air produced the normal results after having consumed some hot cocoa earlier. Just as I opened the outhouse door, having completed my mission, I knocked my lovely warm glove down into the frozen 'nether regions' of the outhouse. That night I learned the true definition of chivalry from my Mennonite young man. Without hesitation he went back into that outhouse, flashlight in hand and retrieved my glove. It never occurred to me that his gallantry was a sure sign that he was 'sweet' on me. Fifty years later his wife passed on that little fact about her husband, now a well-known and revered academic, who shall remain nameless for his own sake.

'Three older brothers—a gift that keeps on giving and lasts a lifetime'

Growing up in a family of boys as I did, is usually a rough and tumble experience physically and emotionally. That was certainly true in my case with lots of name-calling, nasty verbal innuendos, pushing, and shoving. I didn't really appreciate my brothers until I became an adult and discovered what fine men they are.

PETER took on the eldest, responsible, nurturing role even when he was quite a young boy. Typically he deviated somewhat from that during his teen years but slid back into that niche when he entered his early twenties and he has continued to do so. He is exceptionally dear to me as he continues his oversight of the lives of his siblings. Peter and Rose have given us three sons to enjoy, Ryan, Jason and Jake. Peter's compassionate care for our Mom during her last years in the Menno Hospital in Abbotsford was exceptional; day after date he positioned himself by her bedside to feed her. I look forward to seeing his glistening crown in heaven one day!

HERMAN'S personality was most like my Mom's. His exterior fun-loving nature covered his natural reserve. Unfortunately, for most of his adult life, in his married life, he and Helen have lived in Winnipeg, two thousand miles away. Bonding relationships as adults are difficult to conceive when distance separates and in the years of raising children, visits between our two families were rare. Our son Kyle and his wife Kirsten spent a few years going to the University of Winnipeg. While there, Herman proved himself to be extraordinarily kind to them, being the substitute dad that Kyle could count on when needing to deal with frozen water pipes, flooded basements or missing house keys. Proof of his fatherly nurturing is the relationship he has with his children Michelle, Curtis, and Karalyn. Regardless of how old they are, Herman and Helen's home is the default haven for their children and grandchildren. His life-long career with the Children and Family Services slice of the Winnipeg Social Services is comment enough as to his gift of being a people helper and a care-giver. He is a wonderfully kind, empathetic and accepting brother, especially dear to me.

DAVID'S personality, in many aspects, mirrored that of my Dad. David's call to be a pastor came early in his life and for many years he served the Mennonite church in that capacity. Before he was sixty a debilitating illness required his resignation as Pastor in Plum Coulee, Manitoba. However, David continued to be a counselor for many years. David and Lynda have two sons waiting for them in Glory; Marvin dying at birth, and Daryl at sixteen when leukemia proved to be too formidable an enemy. David and Lynda's three surviving children Elwyn, Cynthia, and Marlin are a reflection of David's love for his Heavenly Father. He is known by many in southern Manitoba for his life of prayer, his walk with God, and his compassion for those he meets.

David and I tend to see the ways of God similarly...his singular focus on the Jesus he loves certainly sharpens his view of God. Although now he is physically compromised, he has not lost his quirky sense of humor which continues to tickle my funny bone. Our relationship is one I greatly treasure and for which I am extraordinarily thankful.

After many, many years of seeing each other only at weddings or funerals, we siblings and spouses met at Waterton Park in Alberta on several occasions for times of reconnecting and re-establishing our relationships. What a milestone in the winding road of sibling friendship those have turned out to be. I remember remarking to Ben that I had forgotten how much we siblings genuinely liked each other as people, not only because of our common parentage. As the Adrian siblings, blessed are we indeed.

Edith, Peter, David, Herman Adrian
Leonard and Anna Adrian, my parents
(circa 1962)

8

SUMMER CAMP

Who would ever think that so much went on in the soul of a young girl?
—Anne Frank

What excitement, Children's Camp was about to begin. I was twelve years old; in the fall I would begin grade seven in the Rosemary Junior High School. But now it was summer holidays and, for the first time, the Mennonite churches in Alberta were sponsoring a Children's Camp at a bible school campus. And, not only were my parents allowing me to go all the way to Didsbury, 150 miles away, I was the proud owner of new white canvas running shoes, the kind that really need to be worn a bit so they would mold to my feet and not leave the familiar blisters. I didn't think I had ever been so happy. And, I would be away for one whole week! I couldn't imagine how much fun I was going to have.

One of the neighborhood farmers had a shiny new car. I was invited to ride with him along with four other girls. The day finally arrived. I had packed my small cardboard suitcase days in advance. Carefully I slid into the car as the driver announced, "We're going to drive with the windows closed, girls. We don't want the dust getting into the car." "Well, this is going to be different," I thought. I was accustomed to having the wind blow through my fingers and hair as I hung my arms and face out the window. The faster the car went, the more I enjoyed the rushing wind. I was far too thrilled with what the day would bring; there was no disappointment in travelling with the windows closed. The driver said he would turn on the fan and we would all be quite comfortable for the three hour drive. Before I knew it, we arrived at the campus and we were shown to our dorm rooms. Quickly I unpacked my suitcase and ran outside to join the games that had already begun.

The five days of Camp raced by. Each day brought new songs, new games, new crafts and well-remembered Bible Stories. Each day closed with devotions and a challenge to follow Jesus. This was not new to me, my parents regularly emphasized that I needed to be 'converted;' that I needed to have Jesus Christ live in my heart. As far back as I could remember I had always been a Christian. I could not remember a time when I had not believed that Jesus loved me so much that He had died for my sins.

Every day was full of excitement. Eating in the dining room was so much fun, sitting at the table and laughing with the other girls was exhilarating. Life could not have been more wonderful. And then, life got even better, I met a boy. He seemed to be interested in me: "could that be true," I asked myself. We barely talked; this was unknown territory for me because I was just getting to the age where I would begin 'flirting.' Having three older brothers, there had always been boys on the farm, but I had never looked at my brothers' friends as prospective boyfriends. They were my brothers' friends who thought I was a nuisance. They couldn't depend on me to not deteriorate into a tattle tale.

Before I knew it, it was the last day of camp. Just as I was about to leave for the ride home, I exchanged mailing addresses with the cute young boy. Oh, dear, what would my parents think? How could I have been so brash? I determined to not think of that now. Sadly the buildings receded as the car left the campus. I had been allowed to peek through a window; been allowed to dip my toe into a world completely different from the sheltered farm life I knew. They had been five days of sustained happiness like I had never known. How could I possibly manage to wait a whole year for another camp experience?

In the small Rosemary farming community, everyone would go to the Post Office to pick up their mail. This was my job during the school lunch hour. There was never any mail for me, just the occasional letter from my grandparents in Tofield, Alberta, and the *Western Producer*, a newspaper which my Dad loved. But, two weeks after children's camp, when I opened the small mailbox door and pulled out the contents, I saw a letter addressed to me. The return address showed it had come from the cute boy I had met at camp. Heart thumping, I opened it. How absolutely thrilling!

So the letter exchange began. Daily I would race to the Post Office, breathlessly checking the mailbox. For two days I would read and re-read the letter until I had it well memorized, then the next one would arrive. Unfortunately the pen-pal friendship did not survive for any length of time. Just a few weeks later the letters stopped. I couldn't understand what had happened. He had said nothing about not wanting to write anymore; I had been getting letters twice a week. Day after day the mailbox was empty. Odd, I thought. I began to mope around the house. At the end of the second week of no letters, my Mom intuitively knew what the problem was. Quietly she handed me an unopened letter addressed to me in the familiar handwriting and said, "You know your father will not allow this kind of thing." My outrage was almost irrational. So, my dad had been picking up the mail! Although I felt betrayed and minimized, I knew my Dad well enough to know he would not change his mind. The new relationship was over.

I was glad Dad had not opened the letter, not because of its questionable contents, but because he respected my privacy somewhat. This was symptomatic of the daughter relationship I had with the father who loved me deeply. He never seemed to give me permission to ask or challenge him about his decisions, or actions. Obviously romance at the mature age of twelve was not to his liking. For my part, I somehow felt it had been a shameful disobedience, indicative of my lack of clarity with regard to appropriate boundaries when relating to the opposite sex. I sensed he would not have been happy to engage in a conversation with me about my first official relationship with the opposite sex. In later years I came to understand my father's theology in that he felt dating itself was appropriate only as a pre-marriage vehicle but not part of healthy, coed interaction.

Time slid by; years later in Bible School I met the young man again; however, the ensuing years had given both of us other interests. Nevertheless, even in later life, memories of camp days made my heart smile.

9

LLOYDS OF LONDON

It was lunch time at school and I had wandered to downtown
Rosemary to check the mail. The postmistress handed me the
large ominous looking manila envelope. I had slid the key into
Box 612, the little door had swung open, and I had found a little
card asking me to check with the postmistress for an envelope
too large to fit into the small mailbox. At age sixteen, in grade
eleven, I had never seen an envelope like it. And it was specifically
addressed to me. What could it possibly be? I wondered. I looked
at the return address. I had never heard of Lloyds of London,
Insurance Company in London, England. I was not only curious,
but frankly, just a little apprehensive. The envelope looked so official. What, in fact, did an insurance company do? It was a bulky
envelope. Slowly I pulled on the end, it opened, a thick sheaf of
papers sat inside.

I decided I would wait until I got back to the school to examine
the documents. Once I was sitting at my desk, I began to read page
after page of questions. I discovered these were questionnaires,
asking me for a detailed explanation of my day-to-day activities.
This was getting very strange indeed. The cover letter requested

that I complete all the questionnaires as quickly as possible so the Insurance Company could proceed with the application for insuring my legs.

Something began niggling in the back of my mind. My brother David was known to think of just this kind of practical joke. Could he really have written to Lloyds of London asking them to insure my legs? How could I find out if he had engineered yet another prank? I diligently filled out pages and pages of the application. I described fictitious mountain climbing adventures, dancing competitions and death defying horseback races. Then I carefully slid the completed applications back into the envelope, readdressed it to my brother David who was in college. I asked him to forward them on to Lloyds of London. It wasn't long before I had my answer back in the mail…yes indeed David had thought my legs worth insuring. Bored at school, he had decided to see how far this practical joke could be taken. His ingenuity and penchant for harmless fun still elicits a grin.

10

HAYING

I was twelve when my Dad told me I was old enough to drive the one-ton truck we used on the farm. Finally, finally I was to be trusted to be careful, drive slowly, not to give in to being silly. Until then it had only been my three older brothers who were allowed to sit behind the steering wheel as they directed the truck to slowly meander around the field between the bales of hay. Once loaded, the hay was driven back to the farmyard. It would sit in rows, high above my head, patiently waiting to be tossed to the cattle on cold winter mornings.

Excitedly I crawled into the driver's seat. Two brothers would be grabbing the eighty pound bales with large bale hooks and swinging them onto the back of the truck. There my third brother would carefully stack the bales into rows, five bales high. It was crucial that the bales were stacked tightly and evenly to ensure the truck's cargo was stabilized. It was an enormous community shame to see a load of bales strewn along the roadside simply because they had not been stacked with excellence. It was an open invitation for every passerby to mock at the incompetence, the ineptness, the sheer laziness of the offending farmer who had been careless in loading his hay.

So there I was, proudly ready to be useful. My brother Dave was in the bed of the truck, Peter and Herman had already thrown one bale each into the back of the truck. One of them called out to me "Come on, move it, we don't have all day." One foot on the clutch, the other on the gas, I gingerly began to maneuver my feet in concert as I had been taught to do. Suddenly, my left foot slipped off the clutch. Unfortunately, at the same time my right foot pressed enthusiastically on the gas pedal and the truck lurched forward drunkenly. In the back, David was clearly was not able to keep his balance at this unexpected jerking; he was unceremoniously thrown backwards, bringing convulsive laughter not only from me, but my two older brothers as well.

I cowered under the steering wheel, giggling uncontrollably. Only when I was able to be self-contained and had cautiously snuck a peek, checking on David's welfare, did I sit up straight. Very carefully, very slowly I made my way around the field thinking to myself Wow, if that had been either Peter or Herman back there, I'd be dead! I knew well my brothers' responses in these kinds of scenarios: David was the safe kind of brother; Peter and Herman were suspect in those years. Adulthood brought out the gentler, kinder sides of their personalities.

11

SHE HAS LEFT HOME

Following my high school graduation I bravely ventured to the Brooks hospital, thirty miles from Rosemary. I was hired, dubbed 'kitchen staff' and so began my life in the outside world. I rented a single room in Brooks, with a hot plate and a bed. A fully stocked kitchen wasn't needed since I ate most of my meals at the hospital. Dad drove to Brooks weekly to allow me to spend my two days off at home. It was a delightful summer; I enjoyed the staff in the hospital kitchen immensely. In particular, I was attracted to a rotund First Nations woman who would settle herself comfortably in her chair to eat lunch and announce, "I'm way behind in my sittin' down." The comment stayed with me and has knit itself into my vocabulary.

The Gap Year – 'after High School you will attend Bible School.'

Being part of the Adrian household brought with it the expectation that, certainly, after High School was completed; each of us would spend at least one year in a Bible School before deciding on a career. (From my father's frame of reference, the definition of a career for his daughter was school teacher, nurse, or secretary; those were my only options). Consequently, my first year away from the farm was spent in Menno Bible Institute, a small school with a student population of no more than forty. It was about fifty miles northeast of Calgary, Alberta therefore, one hundred and fifty miles from Rosemary. It was a perfect bridge for those of us who were familiar only with the simplicity and innocence of farm life. Here the restraints were of a different nature. Dating was certainly not allowed, and yet somehow we managed to pair off as young people have done since the beginning of time. Reminiscing and re-thinking that year, I am ashamed to say that I remember very little of the Biblical instruction. Social interaction energized me daily. I remember being called into the office of the Principal who wondered out loud, what would your father say if he could hear your laughter at school? My mental response was, do you think it would be news to him? My really positive take-away from that year is that I left the school having established life-long friendships.

Almost fifty years later, in October of 2010 we were able to have a Menno Bible Institute (MBI) reunion. What a privilege to re-connect with these former classmates. Three had passed away; five were unable to attend because of health reasons. That left seventeen of us to gaze in amazement at what "the years had wrought." We were so delighted to have one of our teachers, Ed Goertzen join us. Clearly, none of us were left unchanged by our life experiences since we departed MBI. New limbs, new joints, the loss of various body parts and hair, the loss of spouses or children either through relationship or death, all were our collective experience. As each face came into the room, covered with initial reserve or apprehension, it was transformed by a broad, warm smile.

Our foundational commonality surfaced when we, poignantly, joined in a Capella, four-part harmony, singing the songs that had originally brought each of us to faith in a changeless God. More than once we heard the wistful comments declaring a longing for a balance of the new and old songs in the various churches we attended. Although we were all on our own personal journey with God, all were still on the journey. None had turned their back on our common Heavenly Father. We reminisced, laughed heartily, recalled stunts and jokes, and prayed for those who were unable to be there. A weekend that came together with less than two months prior notice will be remembered for the rest of our lives with great fondness.

'Dad, I want to live in the city'

In the summer of 1962 I corralled my parents asking them that if I could find a job in Calgary within one week, would they allow me to stay there for the summer. I did just that; and my parents reluctantly agreed. Greyhound Lines of Canada needed a clerk in their large secretarial pool. The memory that keeps resurfacing over the years is an example of the incredible naivety of this young farm girl. I had been sent to the Greyhound office from the unemployment office. I walked; it was a good ten blocks. I spoke to the gentleman doing the hiring. When he told me the job was mine, I announced that I would have to think about it. Once again outside in the pouring rain I walked back up the ten blocks, found a payphone, but didn't know how to use it. So I trudged back down to the Greyhound telling the patient gentleman charged with hiring new staff that I really would like the job. Does that make any sense? ...not even a little bit!

It was time to fill out the necessary forms; address, phone number, and other identifying information. I didn't know the address of the home of the people with whom I was staying, Dick and Sally Boschman. Dick was an older brother of my friend

Elvera. Even more ridiculous was the fact that when I was shown a phone book (another first for me since I had grown up without a telephone), I didn't realize that every address in Calgary was there…in alphabetical order. Well, how amazed was I.

Somehow, I managed to bumble through that job, and actually enjoyed it quite a bit. I registered at Henderson's Business College in the fall. A good friend of mine with whom I had grown up in Rosemary, Leona (Penner) Bajer and I found an apartment on the second floor of a small building close to downtown Calgary. She was working for Alberta Government telephone before her nurses training began.

Under the large window in our living/dining/kitchen area was an equally large sturdy canopy. Early one winter morning as we were rushing around getting ready for the day, Leona let out a 'Yikes' as did I when I saw what she was looking at. In the newly fallen snow tucked under our window, we could see a set of very large, distinctly male footprints that represented a person who had crept right up under our window during the night. Sleep had been out of the question for our guardian angels the previous night. Although Leona had spent her grade 11 and grade 12 years in Rosthern Junior College, the year we lived together in Calgary— filled with double dating and other activities as friends—cemented our friendship, a friendship that brings richness to my life more than fifty years later.

As well, among the many remembered friends from childhood two more are significant. Mary (Thiessen) Smith, also a close friend whose farm in Rosemary was just two miles west, was in Calgary taking her nurses training at the Holy Cross Hospital. She too is part of my list of those with whom I renew friendships each year. The bonds of Rosemary childhood memories seem never to lose their elasticity. Charlotte Harder grew up one mile north of our farm and now in 2010 we have snugged up on the elastic of our friendship. She has found herself in various communities in northern Alberta over the years but most recently she and her husband Bill Van Bergen have moved back to Rosemary where I was able to visit with her. It's my experience that there is something distinctly unique and intimate that remains forever entrenched in each friendship that begins in childhood.

In the fall of 1963 I found myself riding the bus into supernatural British Columbia; consequently I left Alberta permanently. A girlfriend, Hilda Boschman, a Rosemary native, had just finished nurses training in Calgary. Both of us felt the yearning to spread our wings and Vancouver was just the place for us. Again connecting quickly with other young Mennonite girls defined our social life not only on weekends but during midweek as well.

In Vancouver I spent a year as secretary at an engineering firm. My boss was a leering, repulsive little man, who just about managed to destroy every little bit of self-confidence I had gained. Following that unhappy, but instructive experience, I climbed onto a train in Rosemary, with the destination Gulfport, Mississippi. I would be gone for two years.

I have reviewed that scene at the little train station just outside of Rosemary many times. My Mom and Dad were entrusting me into the care of people of whom they had no knowledge, to a country they knew very little about, and to a political situation that must have terrified them in as much as they were aware of it. I was ignorant of all of those emotions that must have given my parents stomach cramps at the time. Years later our nineteen year old Scott, jauntily waved good bye to us before bouncing onto a British Airways flight enroute to India. He planned to be there for a year, and only in that moment at the airport did I suddenly have insight into the trauma my parents must have experienced. They didn't even have the luxury of a telephone, or even a mailing address until I chose to send it to them. My parents' faith and dependence on God no doubt grew by leaps and bounds during those years that I was gone.

Even they had no idea how naïve I was. I remember a very large, very black, and very kindly train conductor who had took the time to chat with me about where I was going and why. He took it upon himself to tell me, "Honey, don't you all trust no one. You gotta grab hold of your purse and hang onto it real tight or you all ain't gonna git to Mississippi no-how. Chil, I don't know who would let you out of their sight this long."

Mennonite Church Missions and Services had a voluntary service program to facilitate the fulfillment of the desires of young people who wanted to voluntarily extend themselves to the economically needy around the world. In Mississippi their program consisted of undergirding the local Black churches with Bible studies, Daily Vacation Bible Schools for children, College and Career evenings, and supervising activities in community centers. I spent two very formative years in Gulfport, interacting with George and Helene Dick, Orlo and Edna Kaufman, and Harold and Rosella Regier who were the long-term workers in Mississippi. These couples were salt of the earth people of God, invested in the work there. Each one became a mentor to me in an area of my life that was lacking.

'The privilege of being invited to stand on the shoulders of others.'

Orlo Kaufman took very seriously the responsibility of leading the team. His reputation in the community was pure gold. He was thought of highly by the local law enforcement, the Klu Klux Klan, the civil rights workers, and the community leaders, as well as the larger Mennonite Conference. He was a gentle man who never swayed from his personal standards and who took every complaint or suggestion seriously. I had deep affection for him and for his wife Edna. Kansas obituary reports of the very large funeral services held for both Orlo and Edna as they graduated into Glory support their reputations of Godly excellence.

Harold and Rosella Regier were spending the first few years of their marriage in Gulfport. Harold was assistant director; Rosella found ways to impact young women like me, who came with large watchful eyes and ears, wanting to experience life away from the constraints of small-town and small-church Canada. Rosella was a gracious young woman who took it upon herself to teach us the fine art of transforming a house into a home on a shoestring budget. She modeled thankfulness in all things, forgiveness, class, and social graces at a time when I didn't know there was a correct way to set a dinner table. Neither did I know that every dinner table needed a centerpiece, no matter how insignificant the meal or how many people were dining. Food needed to be respected and given dignity, remembering always: it is a gift we don't deserve. Almost unconsciously I absorbed her attitude of dignity and honor in the role of wife and homemaker.

Harold and Rosella spent many years in Mississippi, making an impact for eternity by sharing the love of Jesus in the lives of the people they served. They are presently in Inman, Kansas, continuing to serve the Lord in that community.

During the second year of my stay in Gulfport, the Kaufmans were released to go back to Kansas for a furlough. George Dick and his wife Helene were their replacements. George was an immensely compassionate man in his early sixties. He had retired from a life of farming in the Midwest, alternately pastoring and administrating mental hospitals. He was fond of telling me, "Edith, guilt is the most debilitating emotion there is. Among the emotionally disturbed, guilt-induced mental illness is more prevalent than any other diagnosis. Don't allow guilt in your life.

If you make a mistake, deal with it and move on. Just don't allow guilt to take hold."

George was very frustrated with the lack of compassion and forgiving grace in the Mennonite church pews. Church leaders would punish, discipline, highlight mistakes, and excommunicate before they would embrace with forgiveness or encouragement. George felt a great deal of pain at the number of believers who were sent away from the one place where unconditional love was preached but not practiced.

He was the father figure who spent time describing the character of my eventual spouse, remarking, "Edith, you need to marry someone who is smarter than you; that way you'll have very intelligent children and you will always be challenged." Mentally, I inserted it on my list of 'Requirements for Husband Material.' I chose to surmise that the intelligence of my future spouse which George noted would be added to mine, rather than the insinuation that I actually had no 'smarts' of my own.

George and Helene Dick became very dear to me, so much so that years later they drove from Chicago to Prince George, B.C. so they could meet Ben and 'vet' him. George was very happy with my choice, as it turned out. The last time we saw them was in 1982 in Medford, Oregon where I was delighted to introduce him to our three young sons. George had been in a car accident, and although his right leg had been amputated, at seventy-five years old he was still full of vigor and joy. He remained a man of vitality until he joined his wife Helene in heaven when he was nearly ninety years old.

'In Mississippi—safety may be an illusion'

The political scene in the Deep South was anything but peaceful. In 1964 three civil rights activists were killed not far from where our Camp Landon was, (in 2010, forty-six years later, one of the perpetrators was finally charged and incarcerated). Even though we were not actively involved in the integration process, I was confronted with a burning cross beside the driveway one evening as I drove in the yard, compliments of the KKK. It was stark and ominous against the back drop of the Mississippi forest.

Our first training session in Gulfport included all the do's and don'ts of the intricate dance of being inoffensive as white people working with the black population, whites who felt strongly about the integration issues, but were not allowed to be overtly fraternizing with the civil rights movement.

I became very good friends with Peggy, a young civil rights worker from the Midwest. We seemed to have many common values, both of us fresh-faced do-gooders ready to initiate immediate and far reaching change into what was a generational wound. We were two very idealistic young adults coming from backgrounds very foreign to the Deep South, and we were dangerously naïve.

On Sundays we occasionally attended a Methodist church where the young minister was pro integration; our own Mennonite church was not. The pastor at the local Mennonite church felt he would lose his most lucrative members were he to allow colored people to attend on a Sunday morning. The visit with the Mennonite pastor would be my first encounter with the pervasive attitude of entitlement to the two-caste system of African American versus white held tightly in one hand with the other fist closed around the inerrancy of the Bible. Naïve though I was, the paradox was stunning.

I remember my first discussion with this passionate young white Methodist pastor. He was determined to make an adjustment in his attitude toward the Negroes. He had grown up literally hunting them in the forests of Mississippi, being assured they really had no soul. That certainly was a 'light bulb' moment for me, realizing how sincerely wrong we can be programmed to be, regardless of our spirituality. He also happened to be single…and to my great disappointment, he remained that way while I was there.

'In Mississippi—Prejudiced—who me?'

As an aside, it didn't occur to me until many years later that I didn't need to look any further than to my own upbringing, my own Rosemary Mennonite Church, and my own sterilized farming community to observe prejudice. I, and many other young Mennonites who were raised alongside me, felt justified in assuming that we Mennonites had cornered the truth about God, and He was OUR God, favored us, loved us to a much larger degree than He did those Mormons because they were a cult—after all, and we were under no obligation to pray for them or evangelize them. And about the Japanese, they were heathens, lovely people, but their idol worship was extremely suspect. It was only many years later that individuals from the Rosemary congregation established loving communication with the peace loving native Indians living in Gleichen about fifty miles north west. In those years, between 1943 and 1961, I don't believe our church had one person come into a new relationship with Jesus who had previously been either a Mormon or Japanese. And we, literally, thought nothing of it.

'Learning how to be a servant.'

Marlene Ens from southern Manitoba, was in her second year in Gulfport when I arrived. She graciously oriented me to the daily routine. I began to spend a lot of time in the office at the camp, typing out Sunday bulletins for the various black churches. Midweek we would spend a few late afternoons and evenings supervising at the community center where the young children had swings and other play structures while the older teens would 'shoot the hoops.' The community center was connected to the only swimming pool. The connections we made there allowed us to carry on a Bible study program for the College and Career age group during the winter months. Marlene returned to Canada after my first year there and Margaret Derksen, also from southern Manitoba took Marlene's place. Both of these girls were wonderful women of God; I enjoyed living in the apartment at Gulfport with them, and albeit at arm's length, our relationship continues to this day.

Summer at Camp Landon brought young people from Canada and the US for six weeks to help with the various summer programs such as Daily Vacation Bible School for the pre-adolescent children and Bible Classes for the teenagers. Whenever young people from various churches, divergent backgrounds, and geographical locations gather around a common initiative, that common experience is guaranteed to create energy as well as synergy. I have found that these same dynamics are not easily experienced elsewhere. I remember lots of laughter, teasing, games, and walks, as well as serious conversations as we discovered what we had in common and what was unique in terms of how we lived life. During those two years I was allowed a small glimpse into a world that had previously been very foreign to me.

'It is the little traits that grow me, change me, mature me.'

My experiences in Mississippi were formative in whom I have become. Through some of those experiences, regretfully, I leaned how not to live life. In an attempt at humor, ill-advised pranks, callowness, and sarcasm slipped out before the filter in my brain had time to put on the brakes. The painful result was a lesson that has not lost traction even fifty years later. Interjecting humor at someone else' expense, I learned, quickly shouted self-centeredness. Sadly I realized when the cloak of self-absorption was removed, immaturity, and selfishness were seen holding hands. There is still an 'ouch' in my spirit when I review those missteps. On the other hand, I saw how endearing self-deprecating humor can be. There was, and is, a magnetic attraction to someone who chooses to ridicule themselves and expose their human foibles rather than the failings of those around them.

Thankfully, through many, many other experiences I felt the smile and affirmation of God. It has always been my intent to assimilate whatever I learned in those two years into my own *Welt Anschaung*. Someone has coined the phrase 'two steps forward, one step backward'; if we're honest; it's probably an appropriate description of life's journey for most of us.

'Going back.'

In the years since 1965, I have yearned to revisit the South which I learned to love. The musty, dank smell of the bayou still visits and beckons me during the silence of the midnight hours. The snapping of the jacanas interrupting the stillness; the sheets of rain during their 'monsoon' season drenching me within seconds, seep into my memory vase. The velvet magnolia blossoms beside the massive willow trees with their netting of gray swaying in the light breeze always bring a reminiscent smile. And, I remember the intensity of the heat: diminished only by a large window fan—air conditioners were unavailable—and still Mississippi inserted itself deeply into my heart.

I was able to cross off this longing on my bucket list in 2014 when we followed the Gulf Coast from Florida to Texas. When we drove into Gulfport my heart was pounding. We spent a morning crisscrossing the streets. Fruitlessly I tried to get my bearings to find some familiarity in a community which has changed radically in the preceding fifty years. What was once the 'armpit' of the South has been changed dramatically. Homes that were tiny shacks, unfortunately, still dot the back streets. However, Gulfport is also now a city of flourishing businesses, hotels, and tourist attractions.

As we continued to drive I became very discouraged because I was unable to pinpoint any familiar landmarks. In desperation, but in hindsight it was a whisper from God, we located a senior's complex. I found the front entrance, gingerly walked in, and could see a gentleman sitting behind a desk in an office down a hall. A very pleasant black man, in his sixties, told me that he would be of no help to me in re-orientating me to the community; he had lived there for only twenty years. Sadly, I retraced my steps back to the vehicle. Just as I was about to open the door, I heard him call out to me. I turned: another gentleman had joined him.

This gentleman was probably in his mid-fifties—and to my great joy, and with a broad smile—he shared the fact that the ministries of Camp Langdon were central to his growing up. He remembered the yellow bus which brought him to Camp Langdon for Bible classes; he remembered the Community Center where he became proficient at shooting hoops as he visited it every day after school; he recalled the swimming pool; and most of all he remembered Orlo and Edna Kaufman. His comment "The Community Center was the only good thing I remember from growing up" warmed my heart. Although many physical structures from 1964 were gone or renovated the supernatural foundational building of God that grew in this man's heart was not diminished.

The two years spent sharing life with the people of the Deep South certainly changed my life's perspective. My mind has taken me back there many, many times over the years, reminding me of life principles that I assimilated during that period of early adulthood. Remembering, I continue to reinforce my stance that God has brought lavish, rich experiences into my life.

"Don't compare your love story to those you watch in movies. They're written by screenwriters — yours was written by God."

— Peter De Vries

12

CAUGHT

The summer of 1966 brought lasting change into my life. It was the summer that a smiling Heavenly Father looked down from His heaven, corralling Ben and me together. We are taught that the Lord orders the affairs of men; in retrospect, we were the pawns in what I believe, was the Lord enjoying His own of sense of humor. Sometimes right in the middle of an ordinary life, love gives us a fairy-tale.

Ben Matthies, was part of a college and career group in the Mennonite community in Vancouver. This group met every week as a choir. The first hour was spent practicing a few well-known hymns, after which the youth would go to one of the many senior's assisted living homes or one of the homes for the physically, mentally or emotionally challenged in the Vancouver area. A few songs were sung, a Psalm was read, a few encouraging thoughts were shared. Visits from this group of 'twenty-something' were greatly appreciated and anticipated by clients in the various residences in which the group led worship. There seemed to be no end of very serious young men who would later become pastors but first took their turn leading this group during their formative years.

Following this ministry, the young people would spend the rest of the evening enjoying each other in various homes. This had become a very popular venue for UBC students as well as those who had found careers in Vancouver. Far more young men had vehicles than did the girls, so it became a jostling match when the cars were being filled with eager young women, all wanting to casually slide in tight beside the most popular single driver. Single young men did not last long; some flushed young woman who had spent the previous week dreaming of just such success, inevitably snatched up the single driver that week. For a young male looking for a date, Wednesday evenings provided a veritable buffet of panting, single young females.

Three years earlier, in 1963, I had become part of this group when a friend and I relocated from Calgary to Vancouver. Hilda Boschman had just finished her nurses training; I had just finished business college. My future sister-in-law, Rose Dyck, a nurse at the Vancouver General Hospital was our one point of contact in this totally unknown, cosmopolitan, bustling city. The world was full of promise. Soon after joining the College and Career group, I began dating a very motivated young man studying journalism at UBC. This relationship continued, even during the two years I was in Mississippi.

In July of 1966, three years later, I returned from voluntary service in Gulfport, Mississippi. My first social interaction was re-connecting with the Wednesday night College and Career gathering--that bubbling world of estrogen and testosterone. There was a new guy in this group. He was one I had not met him before, but one who had the *chutzpah* to introduce himself to me long before the evening was over. He used the very old, and very tired, line "I think I know your brother"; and, yes, I fell for it. He managed to maneuver the seating in his car so I found myself beside him.

During the evening one girl sidled up to me saying, "I guess you're next on his list of girls to date." I really was not looking for a new man to date; my relationship with the budding journalist was not over. In fact, he was coming to Vancouver to see me that very week.

In a seemingly totally unrelated scenario, during that summer, Ben, and two friends, drove twenty-five hundred miles from Vancouver to Winnipeg. They wanted to attend a Mennonite youth conference. On the return trip from Winnipeg, one of the young men suggested a stopover in Osoyoos to visit a friend. The visit was a welcome relief from the tedious drive through the Prairie Provinces. The four young bachelors sat on the beach getting to know each other. In the conversation Ben commented that he was living in Vancouver to which 'Bob,' the Osoyoos resident, replied that he had plans to drive to Vancouver in the near future to visit his girlfriend. Before the three young men continued on their way back to Vancouver, Ben suggested to 'Bob,' that he connect with Ben on his visit to Vancouver so they could double date. Events began to unfold with remarkable precision. 'Bob' arrived in Vancouver to see his girlfriend…me. He would be there for a few days, staying with friends. I had not yet had time to find an apartment so was living with my brother Peter and his wife Rose. As 'Bob' and I were visiting in Peter's living room, 'Bob' went out to retrieve a book from his car. He walked out the front door to his parked vehicle, leaving the door standing open. The phone rang. It was Ben, the new man from the College and Career group; ever so friendly, and chitty-chatty. Before the conversation could get off the ground, I frigidly said I could not go out with him (I didn't say "I don't want to go out with you," but "I can't go out with you.") He responded quickly with "Well, face it that's what I was calling about. Can I have rain check?" Through the open door I could see 'Bob' coming back into the house. 'Sure' I said, dropping the phone back in the cradle as if it were sizzling hot. The visit with 'Bob' was uneventful,

I don't remember any comments about wanting to double date with someone named Ben; it seemed 'Bob' didn't want to share his time in Vancouver doing any double dating. The suitor from the Okanagan did not remain as a part of my life.

The next week—with persistence that I would come to know as part of Ben's personality—the phone calls began. I soon found myself on our first date...a double date to a ball game. By the third date I realized I had been found by the man with whom I wanted to spend my future. Here was a guy like none that I had met. He had trained himself to be, oh, so charming. No other date had consistently walked me around to the passenger side of the car to open my door. No other date would always insist on walking on the outside of the sidewalk protecting one from splashing cars or being inadvertently pulled into a car to be 'raped and pillaged.' Other young men would often forget to open doors for the young woman on their arm, 'not Ben Matthies. Coarse language was never used within my earshot. He arrived on time for our dates, always carried himself with self-assurance and confidence, giving every appearance of being ready to conquer the world. He seemed to be knowledgeable on every subject I could possibly think of. Years later when he admitted, to my total shock, that he really was not the fount of all wisdom, I reminded him that he could continue to "just make up an answer as you used to when we were dating." His clothes were always pressed and cleaned; every shirt matched the pants perfectly. "What's not to fall in love with?" I asked myself. He established his priorities early on; his first devotion was to his Heavenly Father, his future wife was next and his career third. In my mind, when Heaven had opened a window, my Prince Charming had shot down to put his arms around me.

I reminded myself of the comment George Dick had made with regard to my marrying someone, "Edith, when you're choosing a husband, always look for someone who has an I.Q. higher than yours. You will always need to feel like you're being challenged to be better." I think the jury is still out on who has the higher I.Q. but certainly there's been no lack of challenges. Six weeks later I took Ben home to meet my parents. I was not in the habit of taking my dates home, so, my father rightly assumed this relationship was finally taking me to the altar. My red face heard him ask Ben if he could sing like his brother because it would be nice to have a singer in the family. Ben took that as a good omen returning the next day to politely ask my Dad if he could marry me.

Engaged after two months in a turbo charged, expedited courtship, we set the wedding date as January 20, 1967. It would be held in the West Abbotsford Mennonite Church in Abbotsford, BC. Mary (Thiessen) Smith, my childhood friend from Rosemary arrived to be my matron of honor and Leona Penner also from Rosemary was the organist. A traditional Mennonite wedding at that time included not only a sermon in English, but another in German, as well as a multitude of hymns. Our non-German- speaking friends managed to keep their yawns in check during the one and half hour proceedings. Following the ceremony, our wedding recessional Bach's "Sleepers Awake" was very appropriate for our exodus.

The reception was downstairs in the church basement where my father lovingly prayed a blessing over the future life of his daughter and her new husband. Ben remembers it only as a prayer that started at one end of the universe and landed, finally, at the other end. However, the blessing was as lavish as it was formidable and has stood the test of fifty years of marriage. In hindsight we are extraordinarily grateful that my father repeated exactly what he heard the Almighty whisper in his ear.

Knowing someone for four months is not an optimal foundation for marriage in any flavor of pre-marital counseling, nor would we encourage our children to follow suit. Life as Mr. and Mrs. Ben Matthies began as did the roller coaster life God would use to shape us.

Ben and Edith Matthies
January 20, 1967

13

MARRIED LIFE

The bonds of matrimony are like any other bonds—they mature slowly.
—Peter De Vries

We moved into our first home. It was a small furnished basement suite in East Vancouver. We had naively advertised that we were a young, newly married Christian couple looking for an apartment. Unbelievably that was exactly what the landlord was looking for. Ben was barbering at a shop on Victoria Drive, in Vancouver; I was an office girl, working for a company called Chutter Hydraulics. In the summer of that year, the health of my father, who had been ill for months, deteriorated and he passed away on July 15, 1967. He was only sixty-seven years old and had recently retired from farm life. Clearly my Mom had looked forward to many more years together with him. I remember my Mom saying she heard the gossips whisper that my father was tired of life; he just wanted to escape home to heaven. Her experience with my father was so very different from the gossip; she knew that he really wanted to delight in and pray for his grandchildren. Only the oldest grandchild, Peter & Rose's son Ryan, was born before my Dad left us.

In September of 1967, Ben suggested that we move to Prince George. He had been asked to join two other Barbers who were moving north to set up a barber shop at a time when Prince George was booming. Three pulp mills were under construction; the potential dollars danced in our eyes. Ben went on ahead, hoping to find an apartment for himself and his wife of nine months. Apartments were very scarce and no sooner was the local paper published than the hordes of hopeful would-be renters were racing to find a home. However, Ben was determined, enough so that he persevered through an eventful encounter with a guard dog which left him with a nasty gash. He finally found a little studio suite which was part of a four-plex. Having accomplished that, he raced back to Vancouver to retrieve the love of his life, the sooner to begin their new adventure together.

Our possessions, a large console TV, a three-quarter bed and a small chest of drawers barely filled a little U-Haul trailer. We hitched the U-Haul to our beige, staid and rather dull looking '65 Beaumont; and full of enthusiasm we began the five hundred mile journey. We made our way through the majestic mountains of the Fraser Canyon, through the desert valleys of the South Cariboo and finally feasted our eyes on the dark green forests of North Central British Columbia as we drove into Prince George. The rank odor from the Pulp mills covered us like a wet blanket as soon as we drove into the inner bowl of the city. However, we were determined to love this booming city while we there, having decided beforehand that we would certainly stay no longer than a very few years.

Ben would have preferred to be hauling the U-Haul with his previous silver-blue Ford Fairlane. It sported leather bucket seats, a 289 engine size, factory four on the floor; statistics I could have recited in my sleep even years later. This car was Ben's dream come true. Long after we were married I would hear him tell people it was the car that won me over; regardless of how many times I would re-iterate that all I needed was a functional vehicle; just something to get me from point A to point B.

Unfortunately that silver-blue Ford Fairlane dragged a mountain of red ink with it, and this young bride was not familiar with debt. It was abhorrent to me, just as it had been for my father all his life. Very clearly I remembered how difficult the decision was for my father to agree to have electricity installed on the farm since it would mean a monthly electric bill. Debt was an anathema to him and his attitude transferred itself to me. Consequently Ben decided to make, for him, the ultimate sacrifice after my father passed away. My Mom didn't drive, so it was decided that we would sell the Fairlane and buy the sedate Beaumont. Those were the years when young men were defined by the vehicles they drove, a beige four door sedan was a most unlikely definition of my Ben. We had been in Prince George perhaps a year when we had the car painted a shiny dark green and both of us felt ever so much better about driving it.

The apartment we moved into had a wall heating unit which dictated our suite was warm in only one room during a Prince George winter that was not known for its kindness. We quickly began to fill the two rooms with used furniture which was in abundance in the transient northern BC community at that time. Happily, Ben found the barbershop exactly as he had hoped; it was in a small shopping mall, very convenient for men coming in from the bush for the weekend. They asked only that the barber would clear the growth at the top of their head; in vogue hairstyles were immaterial to them.

I found work quite quickly in an insurance adjustment office. I hated the typing since it invariably meant four copies of everything. It also meant working with unforgiving, stubborn carbon paper unlike today's easy backspace computer, erasing, spell check, and grammar correction software. It didn't take me long for me to assume the attitude…"Hey, if you don't like it, then do it yourself." It must have been my lighthearted cheerfulness that kept the boss from turfing me onto the street. So to my delight a few months later a local doctor whom I had met at our church asked if I would be his receptionist/secretary. I happily began working at the medical clinic where I became very adept at saying "Certainly sir, I'll do it right away."

The next big change came for us when, in 1968, we saw the wisdom of buying a mobile home. This was an enormous decision for us; our first big investment. We loved living there for two years until we discovered we were going to become parents and everything shifted in our thinking. The most outstanding memory we have of our time in the mobile home is that of an ominous scent which hovered around our home in the spring of that year. To our horror, we discovered that, in the frozen recesses of winter, the sewer pipe had dislodged itself and relieved itself of its contents on the ground under our mobile! But soon enough, a gentle soul came with a big truck, a big vacuum; and multiple buckets of lime. With a great deal of expertise he resolved our problem and our embarrassment.

'A dream come true, a salesman at last'

Ben had long had a dream of being involved in selling. As a sixteen year-old he worked in the Chilliwack SuperValu grocery store. The salesmen coming in caught his eye. He determined that one day he would be seen wearing a suit and tie and carrying a briefcase to work. When he began working as a barber he and his buddy, Bert Prest, always made it a point of wearing a tie and white shirt while working in the Barber Shop. Clearly that was a different era; since then jeans have replaced the shirt and tie. One day destiny knocked on his door. A sales representative for H. J. Heinz came in for a haircut and remarked that he was moving on to a new job. Ben grabbed the opportunity to change our lives. Within two weeks on February 1, 1969 his dream came true. He began a new job with H. J. Heinz as the salesman he had so long wanted to be. He was actually one of those executive-looking men who walked the aisles of the grocery stores. Along with the new job came a company car: at last we were 'in clover.'

Seamlessly we were able to sell our mobile home and purchase our first house. We had a few months to 'nest' in our new home before October 6, 1970 when our Chad made his arrival. A more naïve, uninitiated young mother was probably not to be found. I recall so clearly Ben's older sister Lil and family coming to visit a month before Chad was born and treating me to a lesson in diaper folding. I had never baby-sat so, other than clinical facts absorbed while working in the Medical Clinic, I was basically without understanding. Thankfully, my Mom came to spend the better part of two months with us. She was of invaluable help to me while I got used to the idea of being responsible for my newborn.

Chad was a delightfully healthy child; sweet, and determined to be obedient. We did get a scare, however, when, at six months old, one night he woke up with a frightening bout of croup. Simply because I didn't know any better, I happened upon a wise decision. I picked up my very sick child and, still wrapped in his blankets raced to the hospital emergency. It was a wise decision, the best thing I could have done. As any Mom knows, and I would become intimately familiar with croup over the years, the best thing for a little one is to take them out into the cool air where the swelling in their throat immediately begins to release. The child is then more comfortable in a very short while. Chad, however, had landed in a very severe case of croup needing to be hospitalized and in an oxygen tent for the better part of a week.

Late in the fall of 1971, we discovered we were going to be parents again. Ben, in the ensuing years had changed jobs and was selling for Langis Foods. Their product line was institutional foods. His territory demanded he be out of town four weeks out of five, coming home on Friday night; leaving again Monday morning. When we realized we were going to be adding to our family we mentally projected in the future. We analyzed what parenting could look like and realized how imperative it was that children be raised with both parents present for the adventure. This was a very difficult decision for Ben; he loved what he was doing. He had harvested "Salesman of the Year" for several consecutive years. As well, being out of town had a certain charm when home meant diapers and crying babies. Nevertheless, by the end of 1972 he determined that he would no longer work out of town but would find work in Prince George.

Kyle was born on June 15, 1972, weighing 9 pounds 1 ounce. However, until the end of that year Ben was still out of town during the week, leaving me with the two little boys. Kyle, who later became the most easy going, sanguine young man one could wish for, used his first months of life to exercise his lungs daily, with great gusto, and fervor. Delivered with unremitting frustration to me, I discovered colic would be the uninvited, constant guest in our home until it disappeared after six months. No explanation given!

January, 1973 arrived. And by now Ben, using well honed, and persuasive arguments had convinced me that he would be wildly successful selling Registered Retirement Savings Plans. RRSPs as we referred to them, were an innovative idea the Canadian government had recently floated out to Canadians, realizing it needed to entice the populace to become more committed to savings plans. The economy was exhilarated; providing tax relief through a savings plan was sheer genius. The idea needed time to germinate in the minds of wary Canadians. However, the ensuing years have proven we are a nation which has evolved into exemplary savers. Our generation of Canadians has no doubt been goaded by the past generation who survived the lean years of the 1930s and 1940s. For us personally, Ben would need to turn in his company vehicle back to Langis Foods. We would need to choose a new car for our own; a new job, a new vehicle and the portrait of success was already painted.

Soon, we were 'in for a penny, in for a pound' as the saying goes, with Principal Group, an Alberta investment company. This was one of many such investment companies, which in later years could have benefited from a financial combustion fire; we have discovered the name still discharges a sour taste in some circles. We would say of those early years, "We were like the homeless snake that didn't have a pit to hiss in." However, God used that early season in the life of our family to begin to prove His faithfulness, as He deliberately ground away at our sense of self-sufficiency and entitlement.

In later years we would remember the many months when demands for mortgage and car payments were imminent with no pay cheque in sight, even while we were straining to see with eyes of faith. Remarkably though, we always did manage to meet our obligations. True to his nature, Ben regularly, with great optimism, assured me the next month would bring the needed windfall… and sometimes it did. Two years later he turned another corner and began selling for Investors Syndicate. Again, clearly, through his eyes, I saw unparalleled success. In fact, it was indeed a time of financial clear sailing, however, after only four months; Ben wanted to change loyalties.

He was persuaded by a very successful recruiter into joining Transamerica Life Insurance Company of Canada; then known as Occidental Life. So began a life-long loyalty to an industry that really defined who he was; a man with an unswerving desire to bring security to his family. This was more of a passion for him than would be the norm, possibly because he was left without a father when only eleven and became self-sustaining from age fifteen onward.

We came to discover that a life dependent on God was as crucial in the business world as it is in the life of the traditional faith ministry. Regularly we recognized that unless our God brought in clients, gave ideas, wisdom and foresight for wise business strategies, we were undone. In ourselves we were short-sighted, making foolish decisions and had the ludicrous inspiration that we were actually the authors of our own success.

It was also during that year we made the decision that I would work in the office with Ben; not choosing a career outside the home. We didn't want the stress of a job which would prescribe the days I would or would not work. Although, job offers and career ideas have come to tempt me through the years, the trade-offs of being unable to meet our sons when they came home from school, or not being able to travel with Ben when I chose to, were never large enough to entice a change in my thinking. As it was, the early years of working together, parenting together and sleeping together created their own tensions and challenges. It seemed for a while that we could write our own sitcom of 'Who's the Boss,' eventually, however, we worked out, what is now, a finely tuned system of 'Who's in charge where!'

A more recent memory of mine in that regard, took place early in 1998 when our oldest son Chad joined us in the business. Ben and I were having a particularly stressful day; I remember saying to Chad that I would like him to leave the room because I was 'about to blow' and he replied, "Are you kidding? I'm not going anywhere, I want to hear this!" Had he been given the opportunity he probably would have been willing to sell tickets for the event.

Chad seemed to feel that seeing the air turn blue would nicely round out his orientation at Ben Matthies Agencies.

Years earlier, while I was ending my last year working in the Prince George Medical Clinic, Ben and I were introduced to Andy Falkenberg. His wife Joyce and I began working together at the Medical Clinic and she invited us to a party which would prove to forever increase the richness of our lives. In the initial stages of getting to know each other, Ben discovered that Andy had an extraordinary gift for selling, as well as being an amazingly intelligent man. The two men began their business relationship when Andy also began working for Principal Group. Now, in retrospect this relationship has morphed into an indestructible forty five year friendship. Andy and Joyce eventually divorced. A few years later Andy introduced us to Karen who quickly found a place in our hearts. In November of 1977, while I was highly pregnant with Scott. Andy and Karen asked us to join them in Prince George for their wedding ceremony. I was most uncomfortable committing to the one hundred and fifty mile drive to drive to Prince George in the dead of winter while just two weeks away from my due date. Karen and Andy decided they would drive to Williams Lake instead to be married in our living room. We called our local pastor to perform the ceremony. Picturing that wedding today, I can't help but smile…Karen's son, Sean, was ten, our Chad seven, and Kyle five. These three boys lay flat on the carpet in the doorway to the living room, their long legs stretched out behind them. Pastor John Balzer, a man who was well over six feet tall, with a booming voice, seemed to have a penchant for mis-pronouncing names. Each time he used Andy's name, he would declare Andy "Falkenberg-er," bringing a new round of guffaws from the floor, followed by uncontrolled giggles. The adults, especially this mother in waiting, had great difficulty keeping a straight face.

Nevertheless, the marriage ceremony was performed; they have been our companions in life; Andy's career has paralleled Ben's. He has been enormously successful in Fort St. John; together the four of us have traveled the globe on the bounty of Transamerica. In recent years we have many enjoyed driving trips or flying to adventures whenever we could snatch time away from our respective offices. Rarely does one trip or visit end without having plans in place for another. Common financial successes (or lack thereof), health concerns, and life's emotional roller coasters that are common to every marriage and every family have solidified our relationship.

'Yahoo, come over here, come to Williams Lake, we'll like you.'

In 1976 Ben was offered the business territory in the Williams Lake and 100 Mile areas. Relational issues were becoming increasingly difficult within the Prince George office. We felt the timing was right to navigate our way out of a progressively tense situation. The move would give us an arena where we would be isolated from these tensions.

Making our home 250 kilometers further south proved to be a very wise choice. Williams Lake seemed to welcome us with open arms. We found a perfect family home over-looking Williams Lake from the south side. Our property bordered on that of the Seventh Day Adventist School. Our older two sons literally needed only two minutes to slide down the hill behind our home to get to the school. There they enjoyed their first three years of elementary school. Ben found it easy to establish centers of influence; he began sharing office space with a general insurance office; it wasn't long before we felt completely and comfortably immersed in the small town atmosphere.

The day we moved into our home in Williams Lake, John and Connie Sales dropped by unannounced to welcome us into the community. Ben had connected with them on a business level a few weeks earlier so they were aware of our moving-in day. Connie, whom I had never met, worked her way into my heart very quickly. She had a "mouth that would make a logger blush," but unknown to her, the Lord had been working in her heart. When she overheard that I would be having a Bible Study in my home, to my complete amazement, she asked if she could come. Within the year both she and John had given their hearts to the Lord and our bond as friends has never been broken. John and Connie have been gone from Williams Lake for well over twenty years but the affection forged in the few years that we lived in the same community has only grown. Connie continues to be one of my best buddies although many miles separate us and many years have ensued. In 2010 Connie and I had a wonderful week in the Sheffield, England area and later, in 2012, our girlfriends' week was spent exploring New York City.

No sooner had we nestled into the community, however, when we discovered, much to our early surprise, but later delight, that we were once again going to increase our family. Years previous, while watching stunned mothers-to-be of second or third children coming out of the doctor's office having received similar unexpected news, I had had the audacity to sneer at their trauma. Surely, by their stage of life experiences, pregnancy should not be a shock of such magnitude. It was now my turn when an obstinate "stomach flu" began to develop tumor-like proportions and our bonus baby, Scott Jonathan, appeared. Born on December 7, 1977, he weighed a mere 10 pounds 8 ounces. A charmingly beautiful baby, with curly blond hair, dark eyes and a beckoning personality, he was determined to fulfill his obligation of being our bonus. We had previously thought we had a complete family. I was delighted to have a third boy; the thought of a girl coming into my care brought an ice cold bath of inadequacy. I had grown up with three older brothers. I had now grown quite accustomed to boxing gloves littering the toy room, to repairing walls abused by hockey sticks, to the wrestling as well as the continual 'near-misses' which are part of every little boy's bathroom experience.

When Scott was a year old I began taking him to Marg Muise's home daycare. It became clear to me early on that this child would not be taking instructions from anyone, so the childcare experience was not to his liking. He insisted he come with me to our office where he would contentedly play with whatever paper was available. However, the friendship that began between Marg and me is without parallel. I have discovered that I am designed to need close relationships; one of my highest personal values has always been to be a trustworthy friend. God was, as always, at His personal best concerning my needs when He brought this soulmate into my life. For forty years Marg has been in my heart.

Life seemed to be bringing us continual financial success, so, in 1979 based on sureness of future largess, we, along with four others, invested in a building supply store. However, interest rates soon began their skyward climb. At their peak, in September 1981, we were paying a rate of 'merely' 25.4% on the mortgage for the store. This astronomical interest rate meant that each of the investors needed to begin subsidizing the store; and indeed to a very healthy degree.

By September 1982 prudence demanded that we liquidate the store and sell the buildings and property before the bank did it for us. Although one partner had vacated earlier, fortunately three others remained to somewhat mitigate our loss. The closing of the store was felt far more deeply by the store manager and we continue to see it as a miracle of God that the relationship between the four couples has stayed strong and they remain among our dearest friends. Financially in a corner, we researched bankruptcy as an option, but in the end decided against such a move. However, it has taken many, many years to recoup what the bank enjoyed from their high interest rates but which became our misfortune.

Misfortune aside, we then arrived at the self-serving life perspective that we were entitled to express our otherwise successful business experience to the rest of the community by moving to a very large lakefront home on Williams Lake in 1985 and relocating the office into the boathouse that was on the same property. We know now that we should just have an adjustment in our attitude toward finances based on our experience with the building supply store. However, humility was not our strong suit during that season of our life. We hope God has been able to bring rationality to our thinking in the ensuing years. The lake house was an idyllic setting for our family, lots of yard room for Ben to throw the football with his boys, a parking area large enough for many, many vehicles, and of course the availability of water sports. All three boys were handed traumatic and life defining experiences while we lived there, matters which I will discuss elsewhere. This property, although perfect in many ways, came with an ever increasing cost. A forced air furnace needed to be installed, along with the ducting which had to be squirreled through three stories. For various reasons the septic tank needed to be discarded. Before we could access the city sewer system, a two pump system along with an alternator had to be installed. The pumps were attached to the pipes covering a ninety two foot lift before they met the City pipes at the top of our driveway. Every few months it seemed a new challenge would greet our monthly budget. Many times I felt we could make our own version of the movie *The Money Pit*.

Although everyone was initially delighted with the location, rumblings began when first Chad and then Kyle left for post-secondary education. The lakeshore property brought with it a long meandering driveway. This needed manual shoveling, morning after snowy morning. The driveway sloped in just such a way that the sun would begin to melt the small skiff of snow clinging to the asphalt after the driveway had been professionally snowplowed. It needed to be hand shoveled. The mutinous skiff promptly turned to ice around three in the afternoon every day. As they were coming to the office for a comfortable tête-à-tête, it became our clients' experience that their hapless vehicle would have an uncalled for, yet intimate, relationship with the lovely white fence dedicated to separateness by our neighbors on the lake. When the clients then arrived at the office, there tended to be a bit of 'frostiness' in their attitude. Ben and I didn't relish many more years of such experiences. As well the cost of continually repairing the obstreperous white landmark was growing into a substantial financial and emotional investment. With the picturesque property increasingly becoming an albatross we purchased a smaller home in the City of Williams Lake itself in August of 1991.

I found it very hard to leave the charming setting. The privacy, the tall poplar trees, the rolling lawn, the lovely beach, the melancholy call of the loons, and the long dock that seemed to go on forever were a huge loss to me. It seems that good times can make one feel entitled to more pleasures.

Within a few months, Ben, who had always had a longing to be an architect, drafted out house plans whereby he could renovate our home and in so doing craft out an office for himself as well as one for his 'main girl.' He completed his plan in short order. The renovation worked extremely well until it was time for Chad to join us; then we were faced with a dilemma since there simply was not another office room available in our home. Had we not believed or seen God's hand at work in our business, we would have been tempted to call it a mere 'co-incidence' when the home next door to ours came on the market. We were able to take possession of it the very month Chad needed the use of his own office space.

Having had the office in five different locations over the past fifteen years, we now have the best of all possible situations. We purchased the home next door to ours in 1998 and converted the main floor to three offices, a storage room, and a small conference room. It is now virtually impossible for Ben, even in old age, to lose his way coming home from work. If he can navigate through the next-door carport and make it up three steps, he's safely home!

Although we have never regretted the choice we made that I not have my own career; I did take a couple of detours enroute. I have long been interested in being a people helper. With that in mind I enrolled in the local Crisis Counseling Course offered by the Canadian Mental Health Association. I found it extremely useful and consequently spent many volunteer hours on the Crisis Line. As well, I worked for a year as Counselor for the Teen Pregnancy component of the Canadian Mental Health Association teaching a couple of parenting courses along the way. Later I took the hospice course offered here; thoroughly enjoying not only what I learned but also the community contacts. Most recently I have become one of those volunteers who cheerfully calls out "Meals on Wheels" while carrying in sustenance to those unable to cook for themselves. It has been a purposeful endeavor of mine to be intentional about being involved in a community which has generously embraced our family for many years.

> It was as if marriage had been a long, complicated meal
> and now there was this lovely dessert.
> ~Olive Kitteridge

Our sons have left us with empty bedrooms since 1992. They would pop in for a visit or stay a few weeks over the years, so we have basically been re-discovering each other for the past twenty five years. The journey has been delightful. Retirement is not part of our active vocabulary. Regularly I hear Ben commenting that, since he loves what he's doing, he won't be shutting down in the foreseeable future. As long as he paces himself and continues to invite me to 'run-away' with him from time to time, I'm contented with his decision. He has been very intentional about positioning Chad to slide into the lion's share of the business responsibility; the overflow blessing is mine in terms of enjoying our life partnership into our fiftieth year together; our 'Third Act,' where we have completed our child raising years, have completed our career building years, and are now able to enjoy our adult children and our grandchildren as well as the life lessons we have learned.

14

REFLECTIONS OF BEN

Do not be anxious about anything, but in every situation,
by prayer and petition, with thanksgiving, present your requests to God and
the peace of God...will guard your hearts and your minds.

~Philippians 4: 6~7

Eleven year old Ben stood tentatively beside the open coffin. Inside lay his forty-five year old father. He was so very still, gaunt and white now; his hair had stubbornly remained black even after weeks of refusing to acknowledge he could not survive the cancer which was eating at his pancreas. "What am I supposed to feel?" Ben wondered. No one seemed to notice him; it appeared everyone was swirling in their own grief. In 1953 society had not yet come to realize that children needed someone to come alongside them to process the loss of a parent. The emotional needs of children and the need to address them was unfamiliar territory. The seventh child of eight, Ben was often not certain how to insert himself into the weave of family life. His older three sisters were married; he had no memory of living in a home together with his three oldest sisters. Ben was a child who felt he was viewing family life from the outside, as an observer. Years later, he would remember times of feeling like an intruder in venues where his siblings felt warmly invited. As young as pre-adolescent, he had responsibility for chopping firewood as well as keeping the winter fires going. In the spring and summer he was accustomed to working on the small farm in the Fraser Valley. In fall, the small orchard of plum, pear, apple, and walnut trees demanded attention. Daily the cows needed to be milked; rats to be evacuated from the chicken coop; his brother's pigs to be slopped. With the death of his father, life was forever changed.

Ben's father, John Matthies, along with his grandfather Cornelius Matthies, step grandmother Amelia, and their seven children immigrated to Canada from the Ukraine. They were part of a large convoy of trains carrying Mennonites during the 1920s. They arrived anxious but determined, fearful of the unknown yet infused with faith. They felt that the God of their parents had brought them to a land of freedom. John Matthies' first Canadian home in the summer of 1929 was in the little, farming community of Carrot River, Saskatchewan. He was twenty-two years old. With his brother George, John began to work as a farm hand in Moose Range a day's walk from Carrot River. The cold blasts of winter arrived, and the two young men made their way north in search of possible homesteads. The Canadian government was deter- mined to populate the Prairies and dot them with viable farms. The Mennonite immigrants were invited to carve out a life on a quarter section of land (one quarter square mile), clear some land, and build a dwelling on it. If they accomplished that at the end of one year, the land was theirs. John found his piece of land in the Blue Jay area close to Carrot River, Saskatchewan. Unfortunately, the land was full of Spruce and Jack Pine trees and a generous portion of Muskeg. In the dead of the unforgiving winter, John began to clear the land with his axe, and whenever possible, pull out the roots in preparation for the spring planting. He was not alone in how he attacked the stubborn landscape. Other hopeful young pioneers around him were equally absorbed. When summer arrived, he would once again find employment in the farms around him that were already productive and continue clearing his own land in the fall and winter when the weather co-operated.

Ben's mother, Katie Buller entered Canada two years earlier, in May of 1927. Her first home was in Lilac, Saskatchewan. Katie spent her first weeks with her older sister Helen who was a little more established in Canada since she and her husband, Henry Friesen, immigrated three years earlier. Katie quickly found work in the kitchens in the surrounding areas where she learned to read English. In August of 1930 she met John Matthies; they were married a few short months later, on December 7.

In the fall of 1930, prior to the wedding, John was busy building a log cabin on the new homestead. Mud plaster filled the cracks in the logs on the outside, inside the two little bedrooms; front room and large farm kitchen were white washed. The work was done mainly on the weekends since he was committed to working elsewhere until he had sufficient land cleared to begin his own farming. The first winter John spent his time cutting and selling firewood. At that time a cord of wood sold for two dollars. Soon the young couple filled their home with children. Four girls, Susan, Elsie, Lillian, Lottie and three sons, John, Cornelius, and Benjamin were born in Saskatchewan during the years 1931 to 1942.

Each spring new hope flickered for a plentiful crop. Unfortunately and inevitably hail pounced fiercely with heavy boots on the fields of wheat or, selfishly, the heavens would deny their rain. In the spring of 1944, John and Katie were discouraged by the unrelenting disappointment of seeing lush crops flattened by hail, or seedlings unable to root because the heavens withheld their rain. Highly charged discussions were held around the kitchen table before John and Katie made the decision to move west to British Columbia. The prospect of a hard work ethic being rewarded by being able to provide for the growing family was the lure.

Preparation for the move west began. The crops were planted in the spring of 1944, and John made the decision to travel west in late June. As an aside, the crop John planted prior to leaving Saskatchewan was harvested in the fall by his brother George who found the planting yielded the first abundant crop the family had seen in many years. John sold one of his cows to fund the trip and boarded the train to British Columbia. In route he was able to sell unique, realistically painted plaster of Paris figurines. The dollars certainly helped. John spent two weeks in British Columbia. Coming home in July the onerous task of auctioning off the farm animals and machinery faced the young family. Posters were put up in the community. The resulting dollars were carefully housed for the upcoming adventure. In August of 1944 the young family spent three days on the train. They arrived in Chilliwack, British Columbia in the middle of the hop season. Two small cabins were found on a hop farm. They became home as the children and adults picked hops for six weeks. Then they moved to yet another small home in Greendale, about six miles west of Chilliwack. In the fall of 1946, John and Katie became the proud owners of the oldest house in Greendale; a house built in the early 1800's originally used as a post office and the residence for the government agent. It was perched on a small acreage graced with walnut, pear, apple and plum trees. A large raspberry patch was soon planted by the Matthies family. Finally, with seven children between the ages of fifteen (Susan), and four (Ben), the family once again was able to feel a sense of permanence.

John was able to find work quickly. As with many young fathers, nothing was beneath his dignity; working as a carpenter, a logger, in a nursery, in the local cannery, and in a power plant. The berry patch began to be productive; Ben remembers the raspberry crop being a tedious experience year after year.

The youngest child, Menno was born in 1947. In the spring of 1948 the BC Fraser Valley experienced massive flooding. Perched on the roof of the barn with his two older brothers John and Neil, six year-old Ben remembers the horror of a wall of water approaching their small farm. Badly damaged by the flood, the farm house needed to be condemned and John began building the replacement the next year. John salvaged all of the wood from one wing of the old home, reusing it in the new structure. Ben`s father placed high value on impeccable building standards; a trait he passed on to his son, Ben. No piece of wood was wasted. Ben remembers with pride being given the job of pulling out, then pounding and straightening the used square nails, ensuring they were ready when his father needed them again. Although only eight years old, Ben remembers sanding the taped drywall seams, his father always ensuring they were smooth and ready for paint. Rebuilding was a slow process; with John using only hand tools, the new structure was not ready for occupancy until 1951, two years later. It was only then that the remaining wing of the old home was torn down. Until then, with the family squeezed into one wing of the two story building, all bedrooms were .shared among the children. The luxury of having one`s own bedroom was unheard of.

Ben`s father was diagnosed with pancreatic cancer a short two years later and died on July 7, 1953. He was forty-six years old. Four children were still at home, Ken (Menno) was six years old, Ben eleven, Lottie thirteen, and Neil fifteen. Life changed dramatically for Ben. Various illness seemed to plague his mother, Katie, who spent long weeks in the hospital leaving the day-to-day farm chores entirely up to the four children. In today`s society Ben and his three siblings would certainly have been dispersed into various foster homes; however, in 1953 life looked very different. With the death of Ben's father, all sources of income dried up; intuitively Ben realized he would need to focus on earning money regardless of his age.

The next year Ben spent his evenings knocking on doors in the small Greendale community selling Christmas cards in winter, garden seeds in spring, and powdered drink crystals in the summer. He remembers this first job with great pride.

Also during these years, Ben made a serious commitment to follow Jesus. Gideon Scouts was an organization similar to Boy Scouts but with a Godly emphasis. Ben loved the Scouts and it was here that Ben first encountered Jesus and invited Him into his life. He remembers this as a time of great devotion; he became a pre-teen zealot. Along with a few of his friends, Ben would corner their ungodly peers, drag the suspects behind the backstop at school, and scare them from hell into heaven. Unfortunately, this season of devotion slid away when he began his farm-hand career and church attendance became a thing of the past. He would not resume this habit for many years.

The next year Ben took over his brother Neil's after school job, working for Len Zink who had a Dairy farm approximately a half mile from his home. This highly prized job gave him work after school and on weekends, and continued for over a year. Ben remembers being given responsibility far beyond his years. Mr. Zink had three farms, divided by the TransCanada highway. Trucks and machinery needed to be moved from one farm to another; feed and hay needed to be hauled as well. Ben was entrusted to not only drive the machinery, but also to drive the loaded farm truck down the TransCanada highway at age thirteen, clearly without a license. The local constabulary were obviously occupied elsewhere, but just as surely were aware of what was happening. In spring, looking forward to the thrill of driving a big John Deere tractor with a hand clutch, Ben would skip school so he could help with the plowing and disking of the fields in preparation for the seeding. Then came the bean harvest. Ben was responsible for weighing and recording the buckets of beans brought to him by individual pickers. Needless to say, had there been parent-teacher interviews during those years, his mother would have been told that her Ben needed to apply himself in school but also to actually be present in order to reach his full academic potential.

Junior High school was not on Ben's list of must-do items; he discovered working on the farms in the Fraser Valley much more to his liking. On summer mornings he would peddle his bicycle two miles to a dairy farm where, at three in the morning and again at five in the afternoon, the cows were patiently waiting for their milking. The cans of milk were set out on the roadside stand by six am. At fourteen years old, Ben looked after the needs of this herd of twenty cows. Despite the early morning hours of peddling his bike, dodging guard dogs and curious rats, he quite enjoyed the job.

The next year, while in Grade eight, Ben was working for yet another farmer, Glen Toop. It was then Ben had a life defining experience, one which is seared into his memory forever. During one lunch hour, he along with a few other adventurous young boys wandered into a downtown store, up to no good. On a dare, each pocketed a small water gun. Since he had not been caught by the store owner, Ben assumed all was well. Later that evening, Glen Toop called Ben at home with a sharp, "Get your ass over here right now." His employer had been apprised of Ben's little adventure. Mr. Toop was livid, his face contorted: he told Ben that if he ever heard of this kind of stupidity again, he would take it upon himself to 'beat the tar out of him.' Fifty-seven years later, chatting with Mr. Toop's son, Alan, the two men re-visited the incident. Alan recalled that, at the time, his father had commented that he felt enormous responsibility for Ben. Since there was no father figure in Ben's life, Glen Toop felt the weight of needing to father him and bring some adjustment to Ben's thinking. He could sense Ben was at a crossroads; a young man of great potential, who could easily slide down into a very sad lifestyle. On the other hand, he could also be challenged to become an asset to society. Our amazing Heavenly Father positioned that man to forever change the direction of my dear husband's life.

From the age of fifteen onward, Ben was left to raise himself; making some very unwise choices regarding lifestyle. Finishing school he bounced through a variety of job experiences. He worked in SuperValu, a grocery store, and in retail at Eaton's in Chilliwack. He left Chilliwack and became a welder's helper on the pipeline construction in Alberta and Saskatchewan, then to Winnipeg for a short stint in the Safeway Dairy. He was hired in a logging crew along the Jervis Inlet; he spent two summers surveying during the building of the Stewart Cassiar Highway in northern BC. Finally, he made the decision to become a barber. Completing the training at Vancouver Vocational School, Ben began his new career the day he turned twenty-one years old. It was time to turn his life around. I have often heard him remark that it was only in retrospect that he became aware of his Heavenly Father's physical, mental and emotional protection during those years of finding himself. He had been fathered from on High though he had been unaware of it.

Some of Ben's early years of barbering were done on campus at the University of British Columbia. He remembers this as an invaluable learning season. His eyes were opened to the world of influential people, John Diefenbaker, David Suzuki, Pat McGeer, the University Dean, among others. He found each of them to be great conversationalists and very unassuming. This gave Ben the opportunity to hone his own people skills. Gone was his intimidation for those occupying influential positions or who were power brokers. This would be reflected years later in his successful life Insurance career. In retrospect, each work experience was a rung in the ladder of his future life. He was filling his mental basket with knowledge, tools, inter-personal relationship skills, and character refinement. Through the ensuing years, Ben has often dipped back into that basket to refresh what he assimilated then.

Working at SuperValu grocery as a sixteen year-old, Ben remembers seeing smartly dressed salesmen, complete with suit-and-tie walking the aisles of the store. Ben found himself dreaming of filling their shoes. He visualized how successful he would be. And as surely as night follows day, ten years later while living in Prince George, he was doing exactly that. He loved it every bit as much as he had envisioned.

One further defining influence came into Ben's life; he met Iola Feast. Iola became his landlady during a season in his life when he was eager to be taught refinement, etiquette, and tactfulness—in other words, how to be a gentleman. Iola's husband had died at a very early age. They had been deeply in love; in her memory he remained her knight in shining armor. In retrospect, almost by osmosis, this became Ben's goal. Fifty-two years later,

Ben's respect and admiration for Iola continues. His last visit with Iola found her still vibrant and influential at age ninety-two.

The death of Ben's father influenced Ben's involvement in church and, for the ten years thereafter, he absented himself from that slice of his Godly inheritance. Ten years later he gradually edged his way back toward the love of his Heavenly Father. His older brother Neil, over the years, had irregularly challenged him to reconnect with God. It began with Ben's love of music. This meant joining the church choir; or at the very least, sitting and observing the pretty young women in the front row of the choir. God used that season to insert Himself into Ben's life to the degree that he recommitted his life to the Lord, was baptized, and never deviated again from that commitment. As an aside, neither has Ben's love of music become diluted; to this day he delights to sing tenor in four part harmony. Being the tenor voice in a men's quartet for more than a dozen years is a fond memory of his.

I am sharing Ben's journey with God, following his own timeline and testimony. In 1990, while I was recovering from septicemia, his emotional world came to a standstill and Ben took a dive into depression. His testimony reveals that during those dark weeks the heavens were brass. Communication with his Heavenly Father seemed to bounce back to him, slapping him mockingly in the face. However, one morning while attempting yet again to pray encouragement for himself, God highlighted the very well-known Scripture verse in Philippians, "Be anxious for nothing, but in everything, with prayer and supplication, with THANKSGIVING let your requests be known unto God, and the peace of God which passes all understanding will keep your hearts and minds in Christ Jesus." It was the 'with thanksgiving' portion that captivated his mind; he began intentionally and purposefully to thank God. Daily he filled pages with thoughts full of gratitude to God. Little by little Ben's depression lifted, but the lesson was well learned. Through each difficult experience, the diagnosis of prostate cancer, his experience with necrotizing fasciitis, disappointments in business, and in other moments of challenge, Ben's predictable response since 1990 has been, "Thank you, Lord." It has certainly been my privilege to be allowed to make this journey with him.

In everything give thanks for this is the will of God for you.
—1 Thessalonians 5:18

Kyle, Chad, Scott and Ben Matthies

So, there's these three boys.
They kinda stole my heart,
They call me "Mom."

15

OUR THREE SONS

The most daunting assignment in my life began in 1970 when our first son was born. What could God possibly have been thinking when He entrusted first one life, then two; and, then finally, throwing all caution to the winds, yet another son was gingerly laid in my arms. I guess the larger question is: did He actually have the confidence that we would grow these children into adults who had the capability of successfully maneuvering through life? Since one doesn't have an internship for this life-long process, and I was so ill-equipped to be a parent, the Lord knew He needed to be especially gracious to me

Sometimes I visualize the conversation God the Father would have had with His Son, "What do you think, Son, do we dare give those two some kids?" And Jesus would have said "Pretty iffy isn't it? I mean what do they know about being parents?" God's response could have been, "Obviously perfect parenting doesn't necessarily translate into perfect children; look at My kids. I think I'm doing a pretty well perfect job of parenting them, and what a rebellious bunch they've turned out to be."

Then I wonder too, how many of us, given the option, would thrust our children back to their Creator when, along with the gratuitous gush of vomit on our new 'to die for' outfit we hear, yet again, "I hate you, Mommy." The pain of the "I'll never love you again" vanishes in a moment…and the Mommy truly cannot remember it again. Therein lays the mystery! Following that thought process, I realize this is an unachievable calling and it could really be no other way. Isn't that exactly how our Heavenly Father manages to, supernaturally, forget our insulting attitudes, our obstreperous, habitual "I'll do it my way, thanks very much. I don't really need Your help on this one." Too often I've draped the cloak of self-sufficiency over my shoulders, only to see the tatters slide off following yet another debacle that I, with my self-absorbed attitude, hadn't foreseen.

Since one doesn't have an internship for this life long process, and I was blissfully ignorant of the finer points of being a parent. Chad's pliable nature made him a delightful infant. Our obstetrician did a fine job delivering this 8 pound 14 ounce child; decreeing we had his blessing to go into full-time production. My one memory of that seemingly never-ending adventure of giving birth was the anesthesiologist singing Pia Jesu while administering the spinal; and then I was sinking into the warm arms of unawareness.

CHAD BENJAMIN was given to us on October 6, 1970 straight from Heaven where he'd been sitting on a bench swinging his

legs, waiting for his turn to leave. Fortunately for him, he came with a high pain tolerance, physically and emotionally. When God fashioned Chad's DNA he probably realized the oldest child is the one that parents use for practice, so that child has to be thick skinned. Chad was a healthy child with the exception of having a tendency to frighten his mother when he succumbed to bouts of croup every winter.

Ben and I were, and are, so very proud of our first son. In his early to adolescent years we found raising him to be a breeze. Asking us for advice was second nature to him; as was his cooperating with every intention of ours. At sixteen however, we realized we hadn't done him any favor by giving him the asked for advice. Making his own decisions, then living with the results was the price he had to pay for our neglect. Had we had the good sense to see that eventual outcome, we probably would have removed ourselves from his decision making process early on.

Today however, with a couple of decades of working through that impediment, Chad comfortably fits into his character of moral strength, integrity, kindness, and thoughtfulness. He's able to send those mysterious "I know you'll like me" vibes to children. Consequently they sidle up to him in any crowd. No one can rival his relationship with his nieces and nephews. Judah, Scott's oldest son, at seven years old would, most commonly, record in his school journal: "I can hardly wait for Uncle Chad to come this weekend." Predictably, Chad's involvement with Big Brothers has been a natural fit for years, and following that he now invests himself in the Child Development Center.

He has always set a very high bar for the behavior of those around him. Those who treat others thoughtlessly—men who disdain their female partner, or parents who are unjustifiably harsh with their children—are a huge source of frustration to him. He has little tolerance for those whose lifestyle is incongruent with their faith talk.

Although equally loved by all three boys, Chad seemed especially close to his Oma, my mother. The two of them had an emotional connection, the depth of which seemed to elude our other two sons. Probably this was because, in his adult life, he lived geographically closer to Abbotsford he was able to spend more time with her. Chad would sit for hours playing table games with my Mom and her friends who all thought he was just about as perfect a grandson as could be found. Those intimate times with his Oma are probably his fondest memories. Her death when he was thirty-four was an enormous loss to him and, not surprisingly, in the following years, he would comment how frequently she would appear in his dreams.

A few traumatic events in his growing up years stand out in my memory. In grade five he appeared at the kitchen door with Kyle, his panicked younger brother crashing in ahead of him. It seems he had a front tooth knocked out playing the childhood game "Red rover, red rover, come right on over. Unfortunately, because his mother was unaware of the need to keep the tooth moist so it could adhere itself again, his visits to the orthodontist began much earlier for him than for most children.

At thirteen, Chad joined a number of the local youth-on-a-tube expedition on the volatile Horsefly River. Although secure in his tube, he inadvertently was caught in one of the many snags in the river. The undercurrent was determined to suck him under and he was unable to extricate himself out from under the logs. One of the leaders had wisely decided to be the last in the row of teenagers tubing down the swollen river and managed to free Chad from his potential drowning. Fortunately, I only heard of his near death experience years later, when his savior did the re-telling quite nonchalantly. Clearly, the story didn't land quite so casually within me.

Never one to really enjoy team contact sports, Chad began lifeguard training at our local pool while he was in his early teens. This, somewhat, prepared him for the trauma of a spring afternoon in 1986. While living on the lake, we heard the roar of a floatplane leaving the Sea Plane Base not far from our home. Seconds later we heard a sharp "crack" and saw the airplane dive straight into the water. Chad was the first to arrive at scene, hoping to rescue the pilot. Although two others joined Chad, repeatedly diving into the icy waters, they were unable to open either the airplane door or the window. The pilot died on impact; Chad was given the Governor General's Award for his bravery. Later investigation discovered that the pilot was taking the plane out for its first flight after a period of winter dormancy. He was unaware that a bird's nest, along with the accompanying chemicals from their droppings had so weakened the main cable it cracked within seconds of being strained.

When Chad left home for his first year of College, we realized just how deeply enmeshed the three sons were with their affections. Having left Chad at his apartment in Abbotsford, BC one box of tissues facilitated the discarding of Kyle's tears while Scott flooded another one. Fortunately for Chad his Oma was only a few blocks away from his apartment. I don't believe he missed more than one or two evenings away from her quiet, encouraging presence that first year. For her part, my Mom solidified her values in his life so he has never been without a deep appreciation for his heritage and lineage.

From Fraser Valley College, Chad migrated to Victoria for more post-secondary education, but he has always maintained his claim that he's a 'hometown' boy. He has never had a desire to live elsewhere. He eventually bought a home down the street from where we live.

We were so glad he was in Williams Lake when, in 2006, the diagnosis of thyroid cancer came to him at only 36 years of age. Typically, his response to this diagnosis was stoic. The thyroid was removed successfully, and now, eleven years later, he has had no reoccurrence.

Chad's personality is perfectly suited for when the future will require that he control the reins of Ben Matthies Agencies. He seems to have moved almost effortlessly into the office routine. He has a relaxed, warm rapport with the clients. He has mastered all the technicalities of the endless questionnaires, regulations, and 'do not's' that are intrinsic to the Life Insurance industry. As Ben and I have aged, Chad has graciously been willing to become our go to. Whether it's for computer expertise, heavy lifting around the home, or capably sending us away from phone calls or paperwork weeks at a time, Chad seems to be able to fit in our requests. As parents, if we don't want to shoulder the failures of our children, we can't robe ourselves with their successes either; but it's so very tempting to be proud of our oldest child. Chad carries his father's name with grace; his Heavenly Father knew just who to choose to be our first son.

Jaylynn, Myaleah, Kirsten, Kyle, Lily, Clara, Adrianna Matthies

KYLE ADRIAN was born in June of 1972, weighing 9 pounds 3 ounces. His gift to us, and himself, is his easygoing personality. He has always been willing to be stretched, to try new ideas, new sports, and new learning experiences. He made his way through school effortlessly. Parent-teacher conferences brought the inevitable comments, "Well, yes, Kyle could certainly do much better academically, but you know, Mrs. Matthies, he's a very social creature. He's doing just fine and no one has more friends than your Kyle."

As a toddler, his creative, mischievous nature was what often caused difficulty for his older brother. He would hear his three year-old brother announce that he was about to use the bathroom, and would immediately dart in ahead of him. Kyle would quickly plop himself on the toilet; sit there swinging his legs and grinning.

God gave Kyle supernatural healing when he was about eighteen months old. No longer a stranger to croup, I had found that a hot steamer along with some eucalyptus oil seemed to help relieve the congestion. While Kyle was wandering around inquisitively in the bedroom, he tripped over the steamer, spilling the hot water over both his legs. When he was treated in the hospital emergency room the doctor commented that since he had third degree burns on his legs, we needed to prepare him, and ourselves, for extensive skin grafting. Diligently his bandages were changed daily. However, just three days later, we heard the doctor remark with amazement, "I can't believe how this kid is healing, and he's certainly not going to need any skin grafts." Two weeks later he was free of the bandages and today he has no signs whatsoever of the scalding burns.

Kyle's High School years slid by; countless friends surrounded him as he played rep hockey and soccer. He had numerous bumps and bruises, torn shoulder ligaments, broken fingers and gouges to his body of every description. He became quite familiar with the local hospital emergency room.

In the twelfth grade the Lord intersected his life significantly. Kyle decided to take a six-week outreach to the Dominican Republic with the local Youth for Christ group. In hindsight, I realized that decision forever changed the direction of Kyle's life. Within a week of the fall semester beginning he applied to attend Briercrest Bible College in Caronport, Saskatchewan, a school with which we were not familiar. We deposited him there late one evening, a day late for registration, Kyle had officially left home. We spent the night in Swift Current, and the next morning, our thirteen year-old Scott wrote on the steamed bathroom mirror "I miss my bro…and yes, he certainly did.

Kyle has confessed that his return to Briercrest Bible College for his second year was based largely on a desire to play soccer, rather than a sanctimonious desire to delve into the mysteries of God. Within the first semester, unfortunately Kyle had torn his Achilles tendon playing soccer, and he was forever sidelined from that dream.

However, God brought a new dream into his life, when, in late fall of 1991 he met Kirsten Peter. Kyle was just twenty years old, Kirsten only nineteen. Kyle had undergone a shoulder repair as a result of yet another unhappy sports encounter and was recuperating at the Peter farm just a mile away from the school. On meeting Kirsten's mother, Trudy, I quickly realized we could very easily become knit together with affection, a common sense of humor, and a very similar perspective about life. I love to remind Trudy how she convinced us that these two young people really needed to marry sooner rather than later, and indeed they married in October a few months later. And now, twenty five years later, our wisdom astounds us. The love, support, and respect Kyle has been given by Wayne and Trudy Peter has been an immeasurable blessing to us and a sustaining force in Kyle and Kirsten's marriage.

A German word, *Ubernehmung* (literally *undertaking*), doesn't seem to have a complete English counter-part: a term which describes Kyle and Kirsten's attitude toward life. *Ubernehmung*'s functional definition in common usage is partially gutsy, with a 'sure, I'll try that' attitude. The newly married couple decided they would commit themselves to funding their education by tree planting. They began by Kyle planting and Kirsten being assistant cook. These positions quickly morphed into Kirsten becoming head cook and Kyle as a supervisor.

Previously I had despaired of ever having grandchildren, so when their fifth wedding anniversary was a memory I recommended the 'book' entitled *How to Make a Tiny Little Person in Nine Months with Tools You Have Around the House*. That seemed to galvanize them into action. Adrianna was born in the fall of 1998, Jaylynn in the summer of 2000.

Following one year as a school teacher Kyle rethought his choice of careers. He accepted a job offer which would bring them back to the forest industry in Prince George. Myaleah was born in December of 2002 and before she was two, Kyle and Kirsten discovered they were going to be parents again. Kyle's sense of fun and teasing had not left him. When he phoned a few months into this third pregnancy to tell me they were expecting twins, I was not convinced that he was serious, but oh, yes, he was indeed serious.

It was five thirty in the morning, three months before their due date, when Kyle called from Whitecourt, Alberta where his crews were working. "Mom, I need you to drive up to Prince George. Kirsten's water has broken so I need you to pick up the three girls and bring them back to Williams Lake. Kirsten is already in route to the hospital."

A few hours later the three little girls were in Grandma's kitchen. Kirsten was on her way to the neo-natal unit, Royal Columbia Hospital in New Westminster, BC. Then came one of those amazing times where God intervened, dispensing a miracle, and proving again that His eyes are always on His children, looking for ways to bless them.

Following his wake up call to me, Kyle drove the several hours to Edmonton to connect with a flight that would take him to Vancouver. Only our loving Heavenly Father could have arranged that just as the air ambulance unloaded Kirsten from her airplane, Kyle, in another wing of the airport, was simultaneously getting off his flight. Connecting there, full of conflicting emotions of fear, excitement, joy, and trepidation, they rode together in the ambulance. Kyle was able to be at Kirsten's side while she was delivered of Lilly and Clara. They were two very tiny, but perfect girls, together weighing less than seven pounds.

It would be a full month before Kirsten was able to come back to Prince George and still another month before the twin girls were able to be at home. The older three girls stayed with us for four weeks. During that time our Father Himself must have daily whispered to those sweet little girls; they were so delightfully co-operative, loving, and agreeable, never unhappily whining to be home.

During those four weeks I was waiting for a hip replacement, dependent on the help of a cane, dubbed 'Martha.' Taking the girls to the local beach, stumbling as I waded through the sand pushing a stroller with one hand and clinging to 'Martha' with the other hand brought with it hilarity hard to beat! A fond memory of that month was the number of friends who surrounded me with help and insisted on having the girls come play with their children. It really gave me a new definition of inter-generational friendships and the support of extended family beyond any bio-logical connection.

The following summer, in 2005, Kyle and Kirsten moved back to Caronport where Kyle was offered a position on staff at the College. Although the seventeen-hour driving time from British Columbia to Saskatchewan brought a great deal of sadness, there was a knowing that not only were they walking into a place where their gifts and talents would be utilized, but that all that came from God would be good. That philosophy certainly allowed us to embrace their move with at least a measure of equanimity.

As of this writing Kyle's career is with Five Hills Health in Moose Jaw, Saskatchewan. Kirsten has proved to be the perfect life mate. Her emotional stamina, her caring heart, coupled with a keen sense of humor, is unparalleled. Parenting the five girls, hand in glove with Kyle, is a delight to watch. When Kirsten hears someone bemoaning the fact that Kyle lives with six women, she has been heard to remark, "What's so difficult about living with six women who adore him? Tracing their history, and seeing the man Kyle has become has made Ben and I so very proud.

Judah, Jenelle, Scott, Elijah Matthies

SCOTT JONATHAN was born 1977 while we were still under the misguided notion that having two boys was the perfect family. While I was pregnant I overheard another mother-to-be refer to her unexpected pregnancy as a mistake. I determined never to repeat that comment; Scott was referred to as our 'bonus.' And he certainly has been that. And he was HEAVY....he weighed 10.5 pounds at birth.

As an aside, whenever I reminisce about my first visit to my family doctor to confirm the pregnancy, I am still confounded by being given the option of having an abortion. How can our society allow such a choice to be given to a healthy mother, with no indication that any physical defects might be present in the fetus, no indication the unborn child would ever become an at-risk individual. The option of murder was offered so casually. 'Unthinkable.'

Scott decided very early in life that he alone would determine the course of his life; he refused what had been givens with the older two boys. Life skills such as swimming lessons were refused, piano lessons became a battle of wills; soccer and softball were only tried according to his timetable. By the time he was a teenager however, he was not only an excellent swimmer, skilled in soccer and softball, but an accomplished musician. BUT, he arrived at that place not a day before he chose to do so. Dear friends stayed with us for a couple of days when Scott was an adolescent and were witness to the tug of wills around the piano. They wisely commented to me "If your relationship with your child is at risk because of your determination that he practices the piano, your decision has to be in favor of the relationship." She reminded me of the wise Proverb, "Fathers/mothers, don't aggravate your children." And so the decision was made; Scott was free to love music on his own terms.

Growing up in the shadow of his older brothers seemed to encourage Scott to grow up quickly and to not wait for age appropriate activities. Whatever his older brothers did was just exactly what he was determined to do, only five years earlier. He is our visionary, has always seen his future as having far greater possibilities than we could dream of. When one dream is achieved, he is in the process of planning another. He has the admirable capacity to convince others to join his ventures, to dream with him, and to tie themselves to his goals.

At only fifteen, going into Grade eleven, he convinced us he needed to attend the private High School in Caronport, Saskatchewan. Kyle and Kirsten were in Bible College on the same campus at the time, otherwise I'm not sure we would have allowed him to leave home so early. So, immersed in the pain of giving our youngest to the unknown, we deposited him fifteen hundred miles away which unknowingly prepared us for his further 'other world' adventures.

His success in life is a pattern of how Scott faced and overcame what could have been a debilitating fear. As a little boy he couldn't fall asleep in the dark, he needed the protection of a knife under his pillow at night, and chose to put his bed in an enclosed alcove under the stairway because it made him feel safe. This little boy grew into a young man who heard and followed the call of God on his life to India. At nineteen years old he found a Missionary organization which sent him to Varanasi, India, arguably the oldest city in the world. It is situated on the Ganges River, revered by Indians everywhere as filled with holy water. Seven days a week, fifty two weeks of the year, Indian people come to the river to inter their loved ones. After a rudimentary, simple attempt at cremation dependent on the amount of wood the family could purchase for the funeral pyre, the body is slipped into the river. It is a city reeking of poverty and hopelessness. It was here in Varanasi where Scott spent the better part of a year. While he thought he would be working with the Hindu people, in fact he became close friends with four young Muslim men. Ben and I were able to meet these men when we visited Scott in December of 1997 to celebrate his birthday. They were indeed warm and delightful. Because Scott had already established a relationship with the parents, Ben and I were invited in as well. The immenseness of their 'ask' when we were invited to dinner only became apparent when we arrived in their large home. In the Muslim culture, women were never invited to eat with the men; I was allowed to be the exception. No white woman had ever been inside their home, and yet, Ben and I were ushered not only into the main living area, but also into the women's quarters. There we were shown the bridal gowns for an upcoming family wedding.

The family business was one of weaving silk fabrics. Before we left the home that evening we were invited into their fabric showroom. Hundreds and hundreds of fabrics were displayed in every imaginable color. Graciously the father waved his arm and said to me, "Please, choose whatever fabric you would like. It will be our gift to you." We were much honored.

Scott was quite unwell when we arrived. Ben was able to take him to a local doctor, who, it seemed, was very familiar with the difficulty we in the West have becoming accustomed to the Indian food. We were able to stay long enough to see him, with the proper medication, get back some of his health; however, it's my understanding the debilitating stomach issues still greet him even now, some twenty years later.

Having returned to Canada, Scott continued to finish his under graduate degree at Briercrest. The drums, the guitar, and the Indian people remained his passion. In 1999 he fell in love with Jenelle Holderbein, enlarging the list of his passions. They were married in August, 2000. Their first son, Judah Singh, was born on October 15, 2001. In 2004 they were blessed with a second son when Elijah Benjamin was born. Their family complete, Scott chose to attend University in Prince George to lay a foundation in the sciences.

It would be fair to say that, during that year, Scott was not completely settled in the route he had chosen. The possibility of pursuing his music, studying, teaching drumming, and performing music along with the potential of continuing University education for Jenelle, beckoned them to Kelowna. They moved there in the summer of 2005 where Scott began a half time position at the Willowpark Church in the missions arm of the church, focusing on the large Indian population in Kelowna. He found he was energized by the drum students he had as well as being involved in leading outreach teams back to his beloved India. The call to the Indian people continued; both he and Jenelle formed strong relationships within the local Kelowna Indian community. Under the Mennonite Church umbrella the young family spent a year in India studying Hindi. On their return to Kelowna; Scott began working for the Agricultural Department. In 2011 he was offered a position in Swift Current with the Cypress Health Department as Project Change Manager overseeing the construction a new medical and retirement facility in Maple Creek, as well as a another facility in Leader, Saskatchewan. This, of course, necessitated a move back to Saskatchewan. It was a challenging, yet very rewarding position. When the contract was completed he slid into another administrative position where his job description called on him to oversee areas of education within the Health Region.

After five years in Swift Current, both Scott and Jenelle felt God wanted to move them elsewhere. A position was offered Scott with Island Health on Vancouver Island. It was a big move, challenging in every area. The position was a significant career move up for Scott. Jenelle was encouraged to continue an online Client Services position she had in Swift Current with a Financial Institution. She is able to work from home. Being able to greet Judah and Elijah when they come home from school is significant, something many working Moms can only dream of. Both boys have been working hard to fit into a new culture, make new friends, and join entrenched sports teams. Both are succeeding. They are two extraordinary young men.

Scott is a man who will continually be challenging himself with new opportunities, always trying to mesh his strong musical gifting with his equally strong leadership opportunities and with the beckoning of God in his life. Although they are presently living in Victoria, it would not surprise us to hear, at some time in the future, that they feel called to another city, and another challenge. We sense India will always tug at their spirits. If that is God's way with them, we can only say "Amen."

It's heart-warming to us, as parents, to see Scott's intentional fathering of his two sons into a lifestyle that is training them to become the men whom God has called them to become, with their unique sets of talents. Scott and Jenelle find great delight in being involved with Judah and Elijah as they train them shoulder to shoulder. Ben and I watch them with pride and hearts full of thankfulness to God for their eagerness to follow the leading of God in their lives.

Ben and Edith
2017

EDITH ADRIAN MATTHIES

ON THE NATURE OF EVANGELICAL FAITH

"True evangelical faith is of such a nature
it cannot lie dormant,
but spreads itself out in all kinds of righteousness
and fruits of love;
It dies to flesh and blood;
It destroys all lusts and forbidden desires;
It seeks, serves and fears God in its inmost soul;
It clothes the naked;
it feeds the hungry;
it comforts the sorrowful;
It shelters the destitute; it aids and consoles the sad;
It does good to those who do it harm;
It serves those that harm it;
It prays for those who persecute it;
It teaches, admonishes and judges us
with the Word of the Lord;
It seeks those who are lost;
It binds up what is wounded;
It heals the sick;
It saves what is strong (sound);
It becomes all things to all people.
The persecution, suffering and anguish that come to it
for the sake of the Lord's truth
have become a glorious joy and comfort to it."

MENNO SIMONS
1496-1561

16

SPIRITUAL JOURNEY

What is the Chief End of Man? To glorify God and enjoy Him forever.
—The Westminster Catechism

Our personal stories of faith are on-going, as they should be. I ruminated on God's Hand on my life. There were the 'climbing walls' that He threw up to make me stretch, the deep waters through which He coaxed me. I visualized Him standing off to the side cheering me on when I found myself in a 'hot box.' I believe, all of my life experiences, whatever they were, all were crafted to be beneficial for my growth. I have realized that anything I learn or any personal growth in my Christian walk is not a result of my being unusually astute or my being a quick study, it's solely a result of Jesus being the perfect Teacher for me. Likewise, any maturity that has come in my character along my journey is not due to my being an exceptional follower of Jesus but only because He is an extraordinary leader. Nothing comes to me but that it has first passed through the loving hand of God. The situation is either initiated by Him or allowed by Him as He shapes me into the woman He has purposed for me to be. James H. Aughey muses: "This is one of the sad conditions of life, that experience is not transmissible. No man will learn from the suffering of another; he must suffer himself." In my view backwards, I certainly agree.

Our son Scott had a little quote tacked on his wall in India "When God allows you to be put in the furnace, He has one hand on the thermometer and His eyes on the timer." That would be true of my life. Optimally, I have always wanted to be my own hero, and there is that occasional day when that happens. Other days, when I am goaded by the conviction of yet another failure, I don't find myself on top of the heap.

I'm afraid I left home feeling pretty cocky about what I thought I knew about being a follower of Jesus Christ. And, for the first twenty-three or so years, I sailed along with the idea entrenched in my mind that my salvation was secure…therefore, did anything else really matter? Growing up in God, becoming like Him, wasn't something I seriously considered in those years. It would be much later that I would find out that my God can and does take the life of any person, turn it inside out and use it to build character and lasting change.

At home, teachings about making a decision to become a Christian began very early in life…probably with my first bowl of morning porridge. In my Dad's view, nothing was more crucial than walking through life with an ear to what the Holy Spirit was saying to him. Most likely, by the time I had reached the age of twenty, I had made that life–changing decision a half a dozen times. When, as a child, we had a series of evangelistic meetings, I would 're-choose' to follow Christ…I was never quite sure if the last decision had 'taken' since, in my view, one could never be too certain. There were many people, I had been told, who at the end of their days, discovered to their horror that they were in fact not being transported to the streets of gold, but to that 'other place.' I don't remember from whom I gleaned that particular heresy; but it died a very belated death in later years.

Each day at breakfast our family would listen to Dad read the Bible, along with a devotional thought; and we experienced the evening blessing when the reading of another few verses was the last exercise before crawling into bed. As soon as we were able to read, there was an expectation that each of us take turns reading at the end of the day. Our reading was done from the German Bible and some of the Gothic alphabet was difficult to decipher. One particular verse caused us children great hilarity...and therefore stern punishment. The well-known verse "unless a kernel of wheat (*Weizen*) falls into the ground and dies, it shall live alone" became "unless an orphan (*Weisen*) falls in the ground and dies, it shall live alone" thereby certainly bringing new meaning to the original intent.

Our devotions were a holy time, giggling at this new interpretation brought the predictable frowns and scolding. The evening devotional time was the first to disappear as; one after another we became teenagers and stayed up later than Mom and Dad. Starting the day with reading Scripture was foundational in our home, regardless of what the day would hold, it began with prayer and Bible reading. Now, nostalgically, I visualize my mother, over ninety years old, sitting at her little kitchen table beginning her day with a conversation with the King.

I have memories of a lot of scripture memorization, and, although done in German, today I remember much of it with gratefulness. We would stand at attention, one by one and would prove our worth to our parents through our splendid recitations; they would respond by showing great pleasure. I remember it as a feel-good, sweet time. The brave little oil heater was behind me in the small living room, the wind and snow were boasting outside, my Dad was smiling and encouraging me. Invariably my brother David would be also there, determined to divert my thinking processes with amazing facial contortions so the recitation wouldn't be as perfect as I intended.

Memorizing scripture, although to me invaluable, seems to be one of the childhood disciplines that have been left behind by our generation. I believe though, that we're beginning to realize that scriptural head knowledge, which we have previously derided as unprofitable, does travel down to become heart knowledge simply because God's Word is supernaturally alive.

The time came in my life when I began to seriously pull apart the actual teachings of Jesus from those which we Mennonites have added. For example in addition to the simple injunction of Jesus in John 3:16 "...whosoever shall believe in Him shall not perish but have eternal life;" some Mennonite traditions have added, regular church attendance is imperative for anyone who is a believer. Similarly in response to the thoughts written in 1 Peter 3:3, "Your beauty should not consist of outward things...the wearing of gold ornaments," some Mennonites have extrapolated from this, you shall not wear jewelry or facial makeup of any kind. I found it quite a challenge to find the kernel of Divine truth wrapped within generational layering of rules. It was then that those simple Bible verses which I had memorized years earlier would revisit me. I really wanted to be free to follow only truth. I found it a difficult leap though, to actually continually be sorting God's divine, life giving instructions from that which was in the league of Mennonite traditional thinking.

For example, the very obvious teachings against jewelry and makeup were as much a part of being a Mennonite Christian as was repentance and God's forgiveness of sin. To actually walk in the freedom of knowing that my God was far more concerned with a renewed mind than with the renewed color of my lips literally took years.

Looking retrospectively and objectively at the mental gymnastics that took place during those years, I realize that I had subconsciously decided that, since holiness was unachievable, there was certainly no point in feeling guilty about not achieving that standard. I chose to close my mind to guilt. As long as I could convince myself that I was still a Christian, I found I could live with myself.

Somehow, during that phase that extended in my early twenties, I didn't see any dichotomy between my lifestyle or attitudes and serving in the church. Outwardly I continued to curl my activities around only those that were acceptable among my peers. Appearance was everything; no one challenged what was or was not happening in my spirit. My defining verse in that season would have been Micah 6:8 "He has shown thee O man what is good, and what does the Lord require of thee but to act rightly, to love mercy and to walk humbly with your God." As long as I was comfortable with my standard of justice, mercy, and humility I assumed all of God's requirements were met.

Always having a love of reading, it came to be a series of books that would be used by God to finally drum up a hunger for an authentic faith walk in my life. In the late 1970s the cork popped out of the bottle of joy that God had for me and with it came a desire to walk beyond what I retained from early childhood. God began to woo me into a deeper love relationship with Him.

Catherine Marshall's books were in vogue. I consumed her book *Something More*. I felt a deep connection with her thoughts and I began my lifelong journey of becoming a spiritually renewed woman. Keith Miller in his book *New Wine*, among others in that era, convinced me that I had not given the Person of the Holy Spirit credibility. I had stopped with the salvation message, not realizing that after the 'new birth' healthy spiritual growth should follow. The fact that I had not assimilated this into my thinking was certainly not the fault of my parents' teaching when I was a child. I should have gleaned from their teaching and lifestyle that spiritual growth is critical. I knew I didn't want my spiritual growth to shrivel up, therefore the only option was allowing God to tie me closer to and into the Vine. "I am the Vine, you are the branches. When you're joined with me and I with you, the relationship is intimate and organic, and the harvest is sure to be abundant. Separate, you can't produce a thing" John 15:5.

C. S. Lewis phrases it this way "The more we let God take us over, the more truly ourselves we become - because He made us. He invented us. He invented all the different people that you and I were intended to be…. It is when I turn to Christ, when I give up myself to His personality, that I first begin to have a real personality of my own."[2]

I dipped my toe into the process of squeezing events for meaning, wringing out my experiences in an attempt to acquire God's insight and His wisdom. Keen to learn more, Ben and I became involved in a para-church Coffee House fellowship where we discovered the truth of Ezekiel 36:26 "I will give you a new heart and will put a new Spirit within you. I will take out your stony, stubborn heart and give you a tender, responsive heart. And I will put my Spirit within you and move you to follow My ways."

New teachings, new ideas, new language for praying and inter-acting with God filled my life. Week after week with two dear friends, I would listen to Bible teachers, learning how to slough off old habits, rigid traditional ideas, and rules about the Christian walk in order to replace them with the abundant joy-filled spiritual life. A simple phrase (of unknown origin) took root in my life as, again and again, God began bringing experiences into my life. "If you fix a fix that God fixes for you, He'll just fix another fix to

---

2   Lewis, C. S.

fix you." In other words, embrace the experience you're walking through, don't try to circumvent it.

I meditated on "Don't copy the behaviors and customs of this world, but let God transform you into a new person by changing the way you think" from Romans 12. A gradual but consistent change began to take place in my life. The understanding that, in fact, God could make supernatural changes in my way of thinking was life giving to me. He didn't expect me to just follow a set of rules which seemed to only sap the zest out of life; He wanted to exchange my value system for His and, as a bonus, He promised I would love it.

Dramatic experiences of people being "filled with the Spirit" and "speaking in tongues" were happening all around me. This then, became my dilemma. I knew that I had personally experienced the Holy Spirit. It had been an unremarkable event; certainly it wasn't with the bells and whistles I was seeing around me. And why not, I wondered. Around and around I wandered in this conundrum.

It was to be the first of my times when God accomplished a deep work in my heart without any immediate outward evidence. Only in retrospect would I become aware that something had shifted in my heart, some new perspective of God had gained a foothold, or I had become free in an area where I had been frustrated with myself. It would be many years before I could accept that God works differently in each of His kids, and, with very few exceptions, dramatics would never be the scenario for me. Even today, I believe comparisons among believers to be among the most unproductive, unhealthy and discouraging mental gymnastics we engage in. Much too often a spirit of jealousy is the only outcome. And, following that line of thought, too often we crucify ourselves between two thieves, regret for yesterday and fear of tomorrow.

Also during the 1970's I became involved in leading Women's Aglow. It was a season of spiritual growth, new understanding of faith, discovering aspects of the character of God, and being stretched into a leadership role. Through the teaching and experiences I had with Women's Aglow I discovered a deeper level of worship, which in turn fed the desire I had to know God in a deeper, more personal level than I had previously experienced. It seemed, wherever I turned, God was doing, what looked like, a new thing. Ben and I had wonderfully rich experiences attending summer conferences through an organization called World Missionary Assistance Program. Again we a received new understanding of the function of the Holy Spirit and the gifts of the Holy Spirit, and we were not only refreshed and motivated spiritually, but were challenged to know God better. Certainly not all of what we saw and heard was truth, we had to learn some discernment along the way; that was very good for us.

Without a doubt, the discipline of reading scripture, personalizing it, and writing it out has been the one consistent exercise that has given me life and growth in God. An innocent conference in 1982 propelled me onto a track for spending productive time with the Lord. Beckie Tirabassi, a svelte young woman was the two-day speaker. She had also authored a daily ten-part track for reading and praying. Her organized shiny new binder beckoned me, so I bought in, wholesale. If this young chicky, certainly twenty years my junior, could make a commitment to spend one hour every day with God for the rest of her life, I could bravely start with fifteen minutes.

I discovered to my delight that, indeed, one could spend consistent, rewarding time thinking, writing and talking to God; and the minutes would fly by. I loved the 'praise' section of the little binder I purchased from Beckie's talk: the 'thanksgiving,' the 'listening;' those sections were perfect for me. The only part of the track that I really had difficulty with was the 'confess' section, and of course, that's exactly when I had to face the woman in the mirror. Confession? Who me? Whatever for? Somehow I always managed to skim over "Surely, O God, you desire truth in my innermost parts," "There is a path that seems right unto man," "People may be pure in their own eyes, but the Lord examines their motives"…and so it went. I was amazed at how many ways I could find to circumvent, divert, or detour around becoming real before God. I would do anything to avoid being confronted with my own brokenness—which was really so very silly: who, after all, was I hiding from? The human brain can be amazingly deceptive—slide over Adam and Eve.

One journal entry during that time laments "Dear Lord, in my better moments I want nothing more than to be like You. But there are other moments…so many other moments. Help me to see how very good conformity to Your way really is. In my seeking for You, may I be found by You." Repeatedly I would tell myself:

> Sow a thought reap an action,
> sow an action reap a habit,
> sow a habit reap a character,
> sow a character reap a destiny.
> —Ralph Waldo Emmerson

Other life changing influences became available in the 1990's. Michael Young was our pastor for ten years. He had recently been revived in his faith. He was lit up with excitement and energy, and the gush of visions that came out of him was amazing. He wasn't intimidated by any of the icons of the faith, otherwise known as the old boys' club. Speakers from across North America soon began arriving in our little community; we had conferences with resources unheard of by larger centers. We were taught to understand intercession, generational curses, the amazing comprehensive work of the cross, personal holiness, and a lifestyle of generosity, just to name a few. Our eyes were opened to the contemporary work of evil, the spiritual forces over our community and our authority as believers. In retrospect I am awed by the richness of experience and instruction that has been mine living in this little unassuming and understated community in central B.C.

Personally, I was challenged to examine myself with the same criteria Jesus used with the Pharisees of old and have found myself condemned. I was just as quick to judge as they were two thousand years ago. Someone made a mistake and we, as an entire church community, examined them much like a maternal monkey searches for lice on her little one. A church community where we had all, by the way, conveniently forgotten our own deviations from God's pattern of integrity and transparency. Don't we all subscribe to a mental list of criteria for someone who claims to be a Jesus follower? My list had only those criteria which I probably would never find challenging...

-you cannot be a murderer and still be a Christian,

-a true Christian cannot embezzle millions from their place of employment

-you cannot steal your neighbor's car and still be a Christian

-drunken stupors must not be a normal experience for a Christian

However, what wasn't on my list, but most certainly should have been were 'little' misdemeanors such as:

-grudgingly giving, half-hearted compliments or encouragements

-choosing to think less than the best of others

-complaining

-withholding spoken blessings

-fault finding

-forgetting to give thanks

-ignoring the daily God-given miracles.

This list actually seemed to be endless. In the end I find myself most compatible and comfortable in the group of those who are becoming, where I too need to posture myself at the feet of Jesus asking for His forgiveness, recognizing that true change comes only through the Holy Spirit.

And today, where do I find myself? Without a doubt I have a God who loves me unconditionally. One of my favorite mantras has become—nothing I do will cause God to love me more, and nothing I do will cause God to love me less. Thirty years ago I would have said God was teaching me in two main areas. The first would have been, "In everything give thanks for this is the will of God for you."

The second one certainly would have been Romans 12: "Don't copy the behavior and customs of this world, but let God transform you into a new person by changing the way you think." Many times God has transformed my thinking patterns. Many times I hated what was happening inside my head, times when I was helpless to make the change; times when I was totally undone, incapable to change my negative thought life. As soon as I acknowledged to God where I was at, He would change my thinking...amazing!

Now, over seventy years old, I have added a third mantra regarding my theology. "For God alone my soul (*my mind, my will and my emotions*) waits in silence, for He alone is my rock and my salvation" (*He alone can fix any situation*). Psalm 62:1. In this season of life when I am so tempted to share all manner of imagined profound and deep insights on every given topic, it's good for me to be challenged to "wait in silence." I have often reminded myself of the old saying, 'When I'm wrong make me willing to change, when I'm right make me easy to live with.'

Casting long glances back, I see the faithfulness of God, year after year after year. A little vignette comes to mind with regard to the finger of God moving people and situations in place; the goodness of my Father demonstrated to me in just this one situation of many.

The renewal of the early 1990s touched my children as well. Consequently, our son Kyle, after a few weeks' stint in the Dominican Republic, decided a year in Briercrest Bible College would be a good investment. There he met his future wife, and together they worked in the forest industry in Prince George, BC, knowing it would pay for their university education. While there, Kyle began doing contract work with the Northern Interior Health. This positioned him, a number of years later, to begin working with the health region out of Moose Jaw, Saskatchewan. They made their family home in Caronport, Saskatchewan, very close to where Kirsten, his wife, grew up.

Twenty three years later, in a seemingly unrelated story (but not so in my Father's eyes) I needed replacement surgery on my left hip. I discovered this surgery would require a wait of no less than three years here in BC. After hearing my husband ask our Heavenly Father to please shorten the wait time for me (and I admit it dropped into my ears with a bit of skepticism) I remembered that both Kyle and Scott had expedited shoulder surgery while in school in Saskatchewan years earlier. In the morning I spoke to Kyle regarding the possibility of accessing a surgeon in Moose Jaw. From my first encounter that morning in August to the successfully completed surgery in October, a mere two and a half months later, every situation that would have been an impediment ended positively. Only an omnipotent God could so have orchestrated my life and the lives of all those who touched mine to bring this amazing 'coincidence' to completion.

-Ten years earlier God insured that the prosthesis, used by the surgeon in Kamloops, BC to replace my right hip; a prosthesis new to the medical field at the time, would be the exact prosthesis required by the orthopedic surgeon in Moose Jaw.

-Furthermore, God insured that a new hospital would be built in Moose Jaw, one which required the services of another orthopedic surgeon, a surgeon without a waiting list.

-Therefore, ten days after the opening of this new facility, God allowed mine to be the first hip surgery performed in the shiny new amphitheater. (The new surgeon left the Moose Jaw hospital within two years' time. It does look like God transported him there just for me!)

-He insured our children's home at the time of the surgery would be a fifteen minute drive from the hospital, thereby allowing my recuperation in their home to be an easy fit.

-Only God could have moved my children seven different locations in a twenty-five year period, just to put all of the pieces in place to bless this daughter of His with a new hip.

-He is such an amazing God!

If I were to verbalize one addition to my bucket list it would be the lyrics to the song "May all who come behind me find me faithful." I want to live a life of authentic faith, not to pretend to be someone I am not. To be continually motivated to pursue holiness and a lifestyle consistent with a Jesus follower continues to be my request of God.

And finally, what do I want to hear from Jesus when I come into God's heaven? I want to hear the gentle voice of Jesus say to me, "I prayed for you," as God has promised: "since He (Jesus) forever lives to be my advocate before the Presence of God." Hebrews 7:25

17

CHURCH LIFE

The Church's One foundation is Jesus Christ her Lord
She is His new creation of water and the Word
From Heaven He came and sought her to be His Holy Bride
With His own Blood He bought her, and for her life He died.

Elect from every nation yet one over all the earth
Her charter of salvation one Lord, one faith, one birth
One holy name she blesses; partakes one holy food
And to one hope she presses with every grace endued.

~Samuel Stone

During my developmental years I was faintly aware of a rift between two streams of Mennonite thought, that of the Mennonite Brethren and the General Conference Mennonites. However, I had not personally encountered any overt prejudice. I had heard my father comment that he felt the Mennonite Brethren folk had a deeper spiritual life than the General Conference branch, but even as a girl, it was not long, before I discovered that my father's perspective was unusual among General Conference

Mennonites. Within our General Conference community quite the opposite feeling was far more popular.

Although both Ben and I were raised in the General Conference stream of the Mennonite tribe, in Prince George our commitment was to the Mennonite Brethren Church. This was a default position since there was no General Conference church in that city and I could not envision myself being attached to any other evangelical denomination.

Soon after Ben and I began to worship at the Prince George Mennonite Brethren Church I experienced my first cold slap of prejudice from one branch of Mennonites to another. The General Conference Mennonite baptismal mode was to pour a small amount of water over the head of the baptismal candidate, an act that we termed *sprinkling*. The Mennonite Brethren folk, on the other hand, believed firmly that unless one was totally immersed in water, the baptism was not valid. Therein lay our dilemma. Mennonite Brethren (MB) Church membership in Prince George demanded a baptism that involved whole-body immersion; our baptisms did not qualify.

Along with our commitment to Sunday morning attendance at the Prince George MB Church came invitations to become involved in the mid-week church activities. Leading the youth group, being church Treasurer, and working with Boys and Girls clubs were commitments that came easily to us. However, because of the mode of our baptism, we did not qualify to become church members. One memorable evening the pastor dropped by. In the conversation regarding baptism, he casually remarked "even if you should be re-baptized, you will never be true Mennonite Brethren." Our tenure in Prince George, from 1967 to 1976, was thus a period in which we were not entirely a part of the church community; we were baptismal outsiders.

Our Prince George-Williams Lake worship experiences served as a watershed experience for Ben and me. From my pietistic home life during my developmental years with its youthful naiveté; through my exposure to life in Bible school, the workforce, and intense interactions with mentors who also loved God, I had sought to live in a fully faithful relationship with God. Being the object of exclusion from full church fellowship—like raindrops falling on one side of a mountain peak, or being blown a few inches, to the other side of the mountain peak—sent me tumbling in a direction that I had not yet travelled in my faith life. The life-changing experiences of our worship at the Cariboo Bethel Mennonite Brethren Church[3] in Williams Lake is that story.

In the years since we moved to Williams Lake the particular flavor of stereotyping that Ben and I experienced in Prince George has been suffocated within our Williams Lake congregation. Ben and I have served in the most responsible positions of church leadership or governance in Cariboo Bethel without anyone suggesting that we should be re-baptized. I believe this erasing of prejudice, at least in our personal experience, is a beautiful demonstration of the grace of God reminiscent of the Romans 12:2 injunction: "but let God transform you into a new person by changing the way you think."

God's loving act of erasing prejudice, and the loving response of the people of Cariboo Bethel serve as the touchstone for the content of this chapter. It will be an exploration of church practices in general, music in worship, and congregational practices that have served to change Mennonite worship throughout the past half-century. It will be the story of some of the human struggles involved in the discernment and the practice of discipleship

---

3   Hereafter the Cariboo Bethel Mennonite Brethren Church will be referred to as Cariboo Bethel.

as community; and, finally, it will be a celebration of the goodness of God as He has shepherded our small body of Christians in Williams Lake through intervals of disharmony, and times of estrangement from each other, in ways that allowed the members of the Cariboo Bethel congregation to grow closer to each other as they have grown closer to God. This is a chapter of the celebration of God's work at Cariboo Bethel, a celebration earned through the struggle to sort the threads of Mennonite traditions embodying Biblical truth from the threads that are human constructs which are extraneous to the will of God. Of course, the work of discerning Biblical truth continues in the Cariboo Bethel congregation.

This reflection upon Cariboo Bethel makes reference to experiences that, to this observer, appear to be common to many Mennonite churches, experiences that are common to protestant church life across North America. I do not intend to suggest that the Cariboo Bethel experience is a model; and certainly it is not a formula for the management of worship, or for the resolution of church conflicts, that can be applied in all situations. Rather, I hope that these reflections may serve to affirm and to inspire others in their worship and in their faithful interactions during experiences of church conflict. Most importantly, I seek to celebrate God's graciousness to those of us who make up Cariboo Bethel and to express the gratitude that Ben and I feel toward our church and toward God for His work within us.

The matters considered here are offered as experiences of a single congregation in a small city that is relatively distant from any metropolitan district. Cariboo Bethel Mennonite Brethren Church was established in 1965 during the years when Williams Lake was in its initial growing stages. It was and is surrounded by a large ranching and farming community, filled with hardworking, innovative frontier men and women. Williams Lake served as a resource center for families as far west as Bella Coola on the Pacific Coast and for the many First Nations communities planted west and south of the city. Just outside the city was a residential school which in later years resulted in the migration of many of the First Nations people into the city core.

Initially the church was comprised of transplanted Mennonites; however, over the years, evangelical Christians from many streams of theology have made Cariboo Bethel their home. A current quick count would reveal at least a dozen different faith streams represented in the roughly two hundred thirty Sunday morning attendees. For many, many years Cariboo Bethel has had the largest church facility in the city and has been used as a venue for many community art events such as music festivals, concerts, and other events. Because of its ability to seat over six hundred people the church has also served as the venue for many weddings and funerals for Williams Lake area residents who are not Cariboo Bethel attendees.

There are many people living in the community who have at one time attended the Sunday morning services, the youth groups, or the children's events and, although regular attendance is not their present pattern, they call Cariboo Bethel their church. For many years, the church body was filled with young families and was very transient. Only a small handful of the congregation stayed to retire in Williams Lake. As the years have slid by, however, the community has aged, and there are now several retirement residential options. Consequently we now have a wide spread of ages in the services.

The leadership of Cariboo Bethel has always placed a high value on inter-generational communication and gatherings. Showers for new babies as well as wedding showers are integral to the promotion of conversations and relationships between teen girls as well as those of us now of a certain vintage. Likewise fishing weekends have promoted the same value among the boys as well as older men.

A cross-sectional analysis of the economic status of church attendees would reveal educational diversity and professional diversity as well. A good number of the attendees are employed in the forest or mining industries; a number are small business owners. There are social workers and trades people, school teachers and school administrators, doctors and dentists, ultrasound and x-ray technicians, child care workers and building contractors, politicians and law enforcement officers, and of course, undergirding of all of these careers are the homemakers.

Cariboo Bethel has followed typical trends of North American evangelical church practices, including monumental changes in the last four or five decades. We have experienced dramatic changes in our congregational worship, particularly in relation to the allotted time for various worship activities, to the music, and to the social interchanges in worship, as we have sought to be faithful disciples of Christ.

One-half century ago the sermon invariably began sharply at 11:30 and ended punctually at 12:00 noon. Sunday worship began at 10:00 with Adult Sunday School, and then the worship service began at 11:00. The worship service included not more but not less than three hymns, with the congregation singing only verses one, two, and four. An offertory was mandatory, with either an instrumental or vocal solo, as were two special numbers performed either by a choir, a ladies duet, a men's quartet, or solo voices. This formulaic worship pattern was true of all Mennonite churches of which we have been a part. In contrast our present service is a 'mere' two hours; and we do not have an adult Sunday school program.

The first dramatic change came in the late 1960s with the introduction of the singing of choruses. Initially—with a lot of skid marks—the most daring churches invested in the *Psalter*, a book of choruses. Gradually, as acceptance of the choruses became the norm throughout the evangelical world, projectors and screens appeared to display the lyrics. The choruses burst all norms. Not surprisingly this change was met with opposition—we are indeed a people in need of our comfortable pew.

It seemed that our worship leaders loved to write their own music and that their energy flow led to new songs every Sunday. Gone was the music that invited four-part harmony and where the congregation was able to join together in communal singing. Gone was a time when everyone had access to a hymnbook with familiar hymns. Not only were the lyrics unfamiliar, often the score was not melodic.

In a discussion with a dear sister who felt the change to overhead screens was an abomination to the Mennonites, I felt obligated to remind her that, although we 'sang off the wall,' Jesus loved us equally well during both eras. Inside, I confess, I was not happy with the change but I was very aware that the lyrics of some of the new worship music drew me to God.

The writing of new songs morphed into the writing of songs that were meant for performance, not for congregational participation. The timing of the music was no longer the comfortable three-quarter time and the lyrics resisted flowing easily with the metre of each stanza. Sometimes the congregation was left to observe the worship leader in solo worship to God. The trend became to sing only in unison. As a result we now have churches with congregants who have no knowledge of the foundational hymns or of singing in harmony.

It is wonderful to engage in the freedom and joyful expressions common in the singing portion of the worship service where we focus on singing scriptural truth. However, in dismissing the hymns with their profound theology and their sing-able music there is an incalculable loss to the present and to the future generations. This loss was demonstrated recently in our community when we were attempting to put together a choir for the Christmas season. We discovered that only those over fifty years old were able to read music or to sing four-part harmony. I am saddened that the theology these hymns and the related musical skills will not be passed on to our grandchildren.

Currently, I am delighted see more sing-able music being written. There also seems to be the beginnings of a trend toward less variety in the accompaniment instruments. These pendulum swings remind me that, unfortunately, the church music debate has been given life for forty years shows no signs of dying.

Apart from any reference to churches, secular studies are showing the immense emotional and physiological benefits of singing in harmony. Group singing has been scientifically proven to lower stress, relieve anxiety, and elevate endorphins. Apparently, brain function is improved through singing, melding into a choir and voices being blended.

Changes in the distribution of time for various worship activities and the dramatic shift in worship music emerged as elements of sufficient discontent to disrupt the sense of community at Cariboo Bethel. Moreover the discontent diminished our ability to engage in faithful communal discipleship. As a result of the emotional and spiritual dynamics in the church there was a season in which friendships became strained. Conversations were awkward; warmth seemed to have disappeared among us to be replaced with suspicion, with the fear that one persons' words and actions were being used to control another person.

In the early 1980's we were challenged to take a fresh look at the function of the Holy Spirit in the expression of discipleship in our daily faith. In the fall of 1989 our local church in Williams Lake had a dramatic time of revival. Many of us were permanently renewed in our walk with God. It was an exciting time. During the following ten years, we examined the Vineyard church expression. We invited expressions of the dramatic into our local body; we engaged in meetings where people were "slain in the Spirit" and where dancing and laughter were common. Sometimes these expressions were the result of worshippers mimicking the dramatic actions that had been displayed in religious conferences; at other times they were authentic. It became the work of leadership to discern the authenticity of these expressions of faith and then to encourage the worship or to blow the whistle.

As a new century dawned, our local body took a close look at the fallout of having allowed charismatic speakers and influences. It became a season of self-examination, a time of sorting out what were genuine new understandings revealed by God during this time of renewal. We discovered to our delight, that indeed, in our Body, God had deposited a fresh desire to hear Him, with an emphasis on prayer. We needed to allow ourselves to be pliable in allowing God to speak to and through us. We became aware that through Cariboo Bethel He would be opening avenues to pour His love to the nations. As those charged with spiritual leadership, Cariboo Bethel were bombarded with prophetic voices. They declared that Cariboo Bethel would become a resource center, an emotional or spiritual hospital, and a spiritual watering hole. With naïve pride we had visions of conventions, conferences, and mass mailings. We found ourselves in need of prayers for humility.

"If my people, who are called by My Name, will humble themselves and pray, then will I hear from heaven and will heal their land." In hindsight, we discerned the need to humble ourselves; we needed to see ourselves rightly. God really meant "Ask of me and I will give you the nations for your inheritance." He really had "anointed us to preach the good news to the poor, sent us to proclaim freedom for the prisoners, recovery of sight for the blind, to release the oppressed."

It is so difficult for us to tear our eyes away from the natural world, to see into the invisible world that exists simultaneously. I have often longed for a split-second glimpse of where the invisible becomes visible, the unseen is revealed…just so I can get a glimpse of the angels that have looked after me all these years. This longing informs my understanding of the struggle a congregation experiences in the communal effort to be a faithful community of discipleship; which brings me back to Cariboo Bethel and God's working among us.

We weren't ready to embrace what God had for us. We needed to know that we were no more, but just as, special to Him as was any other local body. Another truth we needed to embrace was the fact that, although God had plans to make us a place of resource and refreshment, it would not come until we could humbly receive His instructions. We needed to divest ourselves of our preconceived ideas of how to do church—not only locally, but globally—before God was able to move and use us. We needed to find a place of brokenness, to be released from our fixation on the physical world in order to see the plan of God which had been invisible to us.

At the time when these matters were becoming visible to us we were challenged by the provincial Mennonite Board to choose our allegiance to them or to the contemporary flavor of doctrine. Swallowing our pride and resentment, Cariboo Bethel leadership firmly took the stance that we would continue to be accountable to the provincial Mennonite Brethren Board. We would choose not to join the herd mentality that called us to follow the current spiritual hot button. It was only then that slowly, almost imperceptibly, the winds of favor within our Mennonite Brethren Conference began again to blow on us. We found ourselves not deviating from our basic Mennonite heritage; we became willing to follow the decisions of the Board; we humbled ourselves and apologized. Today, in the very rooms where as leaders, we were scolded, challenged, and disciplined; people from Cariboo Bethel are being asked to teach, to pray, and to exercise leadership in every corner of the globe. It is not our pastors who were called out to lead globally, but rather those from within the pews. It was those who sat faithfully and obediently listening to God, humbling themselves, admitting their inadequacy and incapability of making any dent in the spiritual dynamics binding our community and our nations. These are the ones that are now serving in places of local and global influence.

As the evangelical church at large has matured, so have we at Cariboo Bethel matured, although, clearly, we are all still on the journey. Life in God is never stagnant. James Ryle has penned this phrase:

Healthy things grow,
growing things change,
change challenges us,
challenge focuses us on God,
trusting God causes health
healthy things grow.

Today, in 2017, we have rocketed through over fifty years of change in the church, some of it coming easily and some with a great deal of bitterness from which we needed to repent. I remember, for a season, feeling like I was part of a family experiencing one divorce after another and being impotent to stop the exits or the accompanying tearing. I would now define the church of Jesus Christ as a group of runaways who are trying to find our way home to our Heavenly Father. We're travelling as a family, a whole rag-tag conglomeration of refugees escaping to the safety of our Heavenly home. On the journey we are learning about getting along as a family, we are learning to trust one another, we are becoming committed to common family goals, common experiences. Some experiences are enriching, some painful. We are learning that it is much easier to get God's approval than to get approval from our fellow-man.

Ben and I are immeasurably thankful that at no time did we feel released to leave our local church body and begin worshipping elsewhere. The churches throughout Williams Lake are populated with those who were once part of us. However, God is again filling our sanctuary not only with more of His kids, but also those who don't yet know Him personally. Amazingly, healing has come in our community; genuine joyful fellowship is our experience with each one who now worships elsewhere. We are now able to participate in the outpouring of God's favor on our people here, and those who had their roots here but love Him around the globe. We are still in process. Daily changes are needed as God shows us new arenas of service; places where we need to repent and take a new road. It continues to be a challenging, deeply fulfilling, and rich journey.

In retrospect, for many years I felt that worship was for me, to make me feel good, to make me feel like I had encountered God. During the charismatic, exciting years of renewal at Cariboo Bethel, the dramatic demonstrations of worship fulfilled exactly that need. We felt loved; we felt energized; we felt overwhelming joy; we felt endless freedom. Our focus was often on ourselves, our needs, our wants, and our insecurities. This introspection seemed to be hand in glove with the secular self-focused, affluent generation of which we were a part.

Perhaps we became accustomed to feeling entitled, self-focused, as if we had the right to "feel good." All of these feelings were far removed from God's call to a lifestyle of pursing the Jesus model of self-denial. Jesus calls us to walk in faith, depending not on our feelings, not on navel-gazing; focusing instead on the well-defined promises and instructions in His Word. Passion does have a place in the life of a believer. We are called to know Jesus passionately and to love Him intimately and personally. I believe we are to be ardent and single minded in our determination to hear and follow the promptings of the Spirit.

Without question the church as we know it continues to be the vehicle God is choosing to tell the nations His story. My ability to sustain my focus on this calling is enhanced by the quote "God has His Church to fulfill His mission" rather than "The Church has a mission to fulfill for God."

In this small community in central BC, removed from extended biological family, the people of Cariboo Bethel have walked with us as we parented our children. Over the years many have come alongside, encouraging, praying, and linking arms with us as we matured together. We have become deeply aware of the fact that it is no small thing to be allowed to be part of a group of people who are committed to supporting our family as our children have grown to adulthood; a people who are committed to our spiritual growth and who are committed to the growth of a common body of believers. We can never be too thankful.

18

LOST SOULS

I have come to believe that we do not walk alone in this life.
There are others, fellow sojourners, whose journeys are interwoven
with ours in seemingly random patterns, yet, in the end,
have been carefully placed to reveal a remarkable tapestry.
I believe God is the weaver at that loom.

—Richard Paul Evans

It became clear to me early-on in our marriage that Ben had an innate empathy with anyone needing a place to sleep, anyone who needed a helping hand and anyone who seemed rudderless. In his teenage years he had spent many cold, lonely hours along the side of the road hitchhiking; waiting for someone who would see the outstretched thumb, have compassion, and invite him into the warmth of a vehicle. Ben was driven by the conviction that, since he had been shown kindness, he should not blithely surge past anyone who was also hitchhiking. My challenge was getting over the initial fear of the unknown and the fear that ultimate harm would come to my children. When I conquered that, we experienced a number of relationships that were not only eye-opening, but gave us insight into the conundrum of hopelessness many people experience. Our interaction with them enriched our memory bank as nothing else could have.

It has been said that our days are much happier when we give others a bit of ourselves rather than a piece of our mind. We discovered that if we truly felt this was one avenue whereby we, as a family, were called to walk out our faith; then we would have to hold all our own possessions loosely; with open hands. "Hurt people, hurt people" is a sage truth we discovered whenever we thought of ourselves as wonderfully, benevolent saints. Tempted to think we should be applauded by those who stayed.with us, the Lord quickly disabused us of that nonsense; reminding us that the Biblical mandate is to be doing it "as unto Him" with no expectation of effusive gratitude. Ben's faith expression was experienced in our home; and I had to learn what it meant in real life, in real time, in our home.

SUSAN: Dinner was prepared and waiting for Ben who was driving home from Prince George in early December of 1985. Earlier that day the heavens had begun to open their backpacks of snow. Now snow was no longer drifting down aimlessly, it seemed quite intent on forming a blizzard. The phone rang. Ben told me he had just stopped south of Quesnel, seventy-five miles north of Williams Lake and was bringing a woman home. She had been hitchhiking and with darkness falling, he felt compelled to bring her home, out of the frigid temperature.

Susan arrived. She was a very smart, sophisticated appearing woman. Her black hair was pulled back very becomingly in a chignon; she was dressed in stylish jeans, a fitted jean jacket and bore a small pack on her back. She smiled shyly at me and in a soft modulated voice expressed her appreciation for being invited into our home. I showed her to the guestroom, telling her that as soon as she had freshened up, we would be ready to have dinner.

Reappearing a few minutes later, she graciously sat down and joined us in blessing the food. Our three boys were entranced with our courteous dinner guest; fascinated with her quiet, peaceful demeanor. Conversation flowed and Susan took part in all the conversations, with one notable exception. She easily interacted with the conversation without divulging any personal information. How did she do that, I thought later, I need to learn how. None of us were uncomfortable, but somehow, each personally-directed question was quickly, yet graciously diverted and another topic of conversation started. When I got up, signaling dinner was over; Susan immediately began clearing the table. As we visited I used every trick I knew to learn something about her—without success.

In the days that followed, from little snippets, I did learn she came from a university town in the east, she had two elementary school-age children; she knew the names of the finest china and dinner ware. While hitch-hiking she had traversed Canada twice, had been raped as well as mugged once in the process and was very familiar with Jesus Christ. She commented once that there was no going back to her spouse after what she had done because he would not take her back. She began a regime of helping Chad with his homework every night just for the sheer joy of watching him learn. At that point we learned she had been a school-teacher. Because of this daily interaction Chad came to have great affection for Susan. Just before Christmas we had a youth party at our home where upwards of thirty teenagers bounced around the house, and Susan loved every minute of it. She helped whip up favorite recipes from her past. Working in tandem with her, serving Christmas treats to the group, I understood clearly that she was not unfamiliar with these kinds of events.

December 24th arrived. We had made some shopping trips into town after which she had dropped several items under the tree for our family. Susan commented she needed to go into the Laundromat. I couldn't understand why, certainly up until that time she had been happy to do her laundry in our home. She insisted and it was then I knew instinctively there was more going on under her calm exterior. When I dropped her off at the Laundromat, I asked her to call when she was ready to come back; I would come get her. She never called and we never saw Susan again. Our children felt deeply betrayed, they had invested emotionally into this relationship. Although the circumstances leading to her experiences with us demonstrated that she was a very disturbed young woman, Susan had never indicated any ill mental or emotional health as she related to the children. Their feeling of betrayal would show up in their resistance when another lost soul would arrive.

Two years later an article appeared in the *Vancouver Province*. The RCMP included a picture of Susan requesting information from the public regarding her identity. It appeared she was also circumventing giving them any personal details. We responded to the RCMP giving them all the information she had passed on to us. They had the same data. She had been found with a dead infant in her arms. Regrettably, we were never given another opportunity to help her. She remains a mystery to us but we remember her fondly. She was a very gentle soul who had obviously lost her way.

CHRISTINE: Christine, a woman in her mid-fifties, came to us approximate a year after our experience with Susan. We all remember her; she had a penchant for consuming raw ginger and garlic, thrice daily. At that time our guest room was on the top floor of the house. In the mornings long, before Christine appeared from the upstairs guest room, her fragrance wafted aggressively before her. Our sons would already begin holding their noses, graphically announcing she was on her way.

Collectively we can't recall how it was that Ben picked her up but I believe she asked him for a monetary infusion somewhere downtown, as well as expressing her need for respite care for a few days. In Kamloops, BC, one hundred and fifty miles southeast of Williams Lake, Christine had been shown the door by an irate husband, as she told the story, and had decided Williams Lake was a better option. Rather quickly she had found herself a boyfriend. She proudly introduced him to us, also a man of indeterminate age and even sketchier accomplishments. He spoke at great length on a variety of subjects, although clearly most often not in command of the facts. We observed this did nothing to deter his pontificating.

It has been said that "hospitality is making your guests feel like they're at home, even if you wish they were," and it was with this in mind that we were ever so hospitable to this particular couple. Fortunately, the boyfriend always took himself home before nightfall so we didn't have to address the issue of separate sleeping arrangements. Because they had no vehicle, Christine would walk to downtown Williams Lake every day, a distance of about three kilometers. She and 'Robert' would, coincidently, arrive at dinner time each day. After being with us for a week they disappeared after sharing their 'tightly-scheduled' days with us. We have not heard from Christine again. Concentrated efforts finally restored the room and the bedding to the clean, fresh scent inviting the next occupant to come for respite.

SHEILA: Ben found Sheila with her thumb outstretched along a stretch of deserted highway just north of Lac La Hache, forty miles south of Williams Lake. She was a delightful young woman, probably just beyond her thirtieth birthday, with the fresh scrubbed face of an adventurer. During dinner we discovered that she had been working in Vancouver for a few years and, feeling trapped in the big city, had decided it was time to change her home address. Consequently she divested herself of anything that would not fit into her little car, made arrangements to live with her friend in Whitehorse, and began her two thousand kilometer journey north. She stopped in Cache Creek five hours into her trek just long enough to use the bathroom. Unfortunately, when she came out of the bathroom she discovered that her car with all her belongings complete with a large amount of cash had left without her.

In our home that evening she spoke to her friend in Whitehorse and decided to stay with us for a day to get her bearings. The next morning Ben drove her to the Husky Truck stop on the highway which would take her north. Once there, Ben approached one of the truck drivers who was having breakfast and explained Sheila's situation. This driver in turn introduced her to another trucker already travelling to Whitehorse. Ben heard him instructing the younger driver, "and you see she gets there safe; you know I'll hear about it if she doesn't." It was so encouraging to see the level of decency among these long haul truckers. Once more God, I believe, brought this young woman into our lives for a purpose and all He asked of us was to extend the same grace we would want to experience ourselves.

RICHARD: Richard came to stay with us for his grade-twelve school year. He had become a very lonely young man since his parents' marriage had dissolved. His father worked in the oil fields in northern Alberta. Now he found he didn't fit into his mother's new living arrangements. He had been bouncing around from one home to the other in Horsefly, a community an hour's drive away. At the time all the senior secondary students from Horsefly were bussed into Williams Lake. The 'magnanimous' school district officials had encouraged Richard to find himself a home in Williams Lake so they wouldn't incur the 'insurmountable costs' of adding him to the daily bus quota.

Our son Scott was in grade ten at the time; the older two boys were in post-secondary schools. In hindsight and to my continuing regret, we perhaps were too myopic to recognize we were not acting in total wisdom or in Scott's best interests. I have come to believe now that Scott would have benefited from being the only child at home for a year. Richard, we discovered, in addition to having a proclivity to porn magazines, had other debatable habits.

We situated Richard in a large downstairs bedroom, large enough, in fact, to house an old TV console and a new puppy which I had strictly forbidden. The room also included a bed and all Richard's personal belongings: a couple of wooden treasure boxes kept under lock and key. The puppy became a source of great frustration to me. I was unaware he was even there for the first few days. I think initially he attended school with Richard but clearly during the late afternoon and evening a puppy that is not housetrained is almost impossible to hide. Consequently when Richard left at the end of the school year, a lot of carpet shampooing needed to be done.

We treated Richard as another son and naively left him in our home to his own devices over the two week Christmas break while we were gone that year. It would only be much later when he left at the end of the school year that we would discover just how much he had, in fact, enjoyed our home. Men's dress shirts, cassette tapes, shoes, a curio cabinet temporarily stored downstairs, had been spirited away. After he left our home other acquaintances of his contacted us and discovered they also had 'given' Richard personal possessions such as a faux Rolex watch, and Game Boys. These, grabbed with sticky fingers, had no doubt been comfortably resting in his treasure boxes. I've come to understand the fact that becoming a kleptomaniac is not an uncommon response from someone whose existence has never been a priority to anyone, most significantly, not to his parents. Richard had never been shown unconditional love by his parents, which is what every child deserves. Although Richard was not a hitchhiker, he certainly was a lost soul.

JOHN: In those years when strangers of unknown origin and questionable intent seemed to rotate through our home, well-meaning friends often challenged us regarding our own safety. With the exception of one incident, we have always felt very much at ease with sharing our home One winter evening, we gathered up a young man after Sunday evening church service since he had commented that he had no place to spend the night. Although he was quite engaging, I was very troubled throughout the night as was Ben. Both of us were up early, anxious to see this young man on his way, which we did right after breakfast. We will never know what we were protected from. Scripturally each of us is promised at least two angels "guarding us in all our ways" and those two may have been very busy that snowy night.

Ben has continued to pick up hitchhikers in the ensuing years although he has not again felt the Lord asking him to bring them home. It seemed to have been a season in our lives where we were asked to share of ourselves. Ben continues to give rides, but only when he is very sure that is what is being asked of him, sometimes doubling back a long distance to pick up someone whom he initially passed by.

DEBBIE For the first time I picked up a hitchhiker in the summer of 2010. She was a woman in her early fifties who had been 'rode hard and put down wet.' Her broken, missing teeth were mute testimony to unhappy, past relationships. As she was fastening her seatbelt, I asked her how she was and was greeted with a burst of tears. She revealed the fact that her third husband was in the process of leaving her.

She had had the gall to have her husband charged with domestic abuse after she had lost two teeth in an altercation with him. He felt the charges most unfair; he should be able to keep his

COME, WALK WITH ME

woman in line shouldn't he? Typically, she was already remorseful about her decision and was in the process of deliberating how she could convince him to allow her back into his life. Dropping her off an hour later, I felt so very grateful for my place in life. I didn't need to be reminded of the fact that this dear lady was no less precious than me to our Heavenly Father. I realized anew the need to always be prepared to pass on the hope, and the guidelines, that God had given to me if I wanted life to succeed in any dimension.

ALBERTA: Driving to Abbotsford in late October I breezed by a woman standing along the highway near Boston Bar. I glanced at her just as the sun glinted off the red container by her feet which caught my eye. So I threw up a "what do *you* think, Lord?" Again the red container bubbled to the surface. "That's probably a jerry can for gas," I thought, "She's run out of gas somewhere." Immediately the 'there but for the grace of God go I' popped into my head. No one has to remind me how often I tempt the gods-of-gas to see how many more miles I can get out of a tankful of gas.

I found a turn off, drove back, sized her up a second time, and then decided she needed a ride. The red that had caught my eye was, in fact not a jerry can. It turned out to be a large gym bag and she, Alberta Chester, turned out to be a delightful Christian lady, albeit a bit eccentric. She appeared to be in her mid- fifties and was doing a survey in preparation for writing a book, saying that she was trying to discover "how Christians lived their lives." Originally from Manitoba, her deceased husband had been a musician spending time playing with the well-known Burton Cummings in his hometown of Winnipeg. She remembered those years with great clarity and so spoke at length explaining the challenges of being the wife of a musician.

She acknowledged that her children worried about her hitch-hiking across western Canada but was confident their prayers for her safety would be effective. We shared small talk as I tried to discern her authenticity...and found her to be exactly who she claimed to be. With the exception of what she could tuck into her little bag, she had divested herself she owned; she was a very gentle woman in search of the calling of God on her life. A few hours later I deposited her in Chilliwack at a service station. She assured me she had friends she would call and would certainly have a bed for the night. Her plans for the next day were indecisive, she felt assured God would tell her where her next destination would be.

I am of the strong belief that no one comes into our life without a divine purpose. This is true of everyone who intersects our lives. However, God's purpose in granting me this last encounter will be fodder for my rumination, and further conversation with my Heavenly Father for some time to come.

19

AROUND THE WORLD

Once you have traveled, the voyage never ends, but is played out over and over again in the quietest chambers. The mind can never break off from the journey.
–Pat Conroy

We have been extraordinarily fortunate to have traveled to virtually every corner of the world, thanks to Ben's business acumen, his salesmanship, and Transamerica's generosity. Each trip was the result of Ben meeting Transamerica's qualifications; for one week each year we were treated like royalty: we stayed in five star, luxurious accommodations and we established friendships from around the globe.

SAN FRANCISCO: Our first convention, in 1978, was at the San Francisco Fairmount Hotel. We were naive, wide eyed, nervous, and certainly unsure of ourselves. The hotel is the oldest, most lavish, and arguably the most beautiful in San Francisco. I had read that really- cosmopolitan women had their hair coiffed in the hotel salons when on convention. Expecting to pay accordingly, I braced myself for the bill and wasn't disappointed. What I hadn't counted on was being disappointed with the outcome. The end result of the hour spent in the salon was no different than my own hairdresser produced.

Huge jumbo prawns, other appetizers, and wines of every description; lavish banquets with exotic table settings greeted us each evening. We loved the Cable Cars, the stinging fishy smell permeating every street in San Francisco. The drive to Muir Woods with its plethora of boutiques and endless fishing memorabilia is unforgettable. The most poignant memory that remains with me is of the first meet-and-greet evening. This memory, unfortunately, is of a 'be sure your sins will find you out' nature. Walking into the conference room, one of the first people we saw was a young woman Ben and I had come to know in our pre-marriage years in the Vancouver college and career group. To her embarrassment she was clinging to a young man who was definitely someone else's husband. The startled expression on her face when she saw us was clear evidence that all was not well. We had decidedly put a crimp in her convention plans. Red-faced, she managed to glide out of the room without speaking to us and did not appear at any of the other events.

As I follow that type of experience over the years that followed, it is interesting to notice how many times that scenario has been repeated, albeit with less and less embarrassment. It has sadly, become very commonplace to exchange the old companion for the new. It was always with a sense of relief that, with a very few exceptions, the core group of treasured couples we encountered at these conventions, stayed intact.

VIENNA: Our first intercontinental conference took us to Austria on a private Transamerica Jetliner. Being of European extraction, Ben and I fell in love again with the enchanting waltzes in Vienna. European music seemed to be around every corner, greeting us at every lavish cathedral we were shown, regardless of what time of the day it was. I found it most interesting that in one cathedral after another we were shown antique libraries, filled with hundreds of historical tomes, yet without a single book about Jesus Christ. It was an exercise in mental gymnastics to ponder the state of the Western cradle of our faith. But it was always the historical architecture which lured Ben out to the streets again and again. The stately, gothic buildings with their glitz and drama totally enthralled him. Day after day we sat in the public piazzas and let the classical music nourish our souls.

MONACO: The following year found us in Monte Carlo, in the small principality of Monaco. It was just a few years after Princess Grace Kelly; the wife of Prince Rainier of Monte Carlo was killed on one of the beautiful scenic roads we toured in the mountains. Even though the scenery was breathtaking, it was nevertheless a sobering tour. The lovely piazza, shining with marble walkways was continually being swept, even at midnight as we sauntered back to our hotel from the open-air banquet hall near the presidential palace. We felt truly pampered, eyes opened wide, at the luxury around us as we were entertained by Frank Sinatra.

HONG KONG: A conference in Hong Kong allowed me to become adept at bargaining, a passion not shared by Ben. In fact, it was a source of much embarrassment to him. It was important to me that I always left with the vendor smiling, both of us happy with the end result; so much so that for a number of years I would continue to receive lovely Christmas Cards from the store owner. Neither did he mind the customers I sent his way.

Immediately following the Hong Kong conference we became part of a small tour into mainland China, when that country first opened its doors to tourists in 1982. We were carefully guided, secluded from all but the officially sanctioned venues. Our tour had been meticulously crafted to be a showpiece of only what the Chinese authorities deemed appropriate for western tourists. We quickly discovered that when an inappropriate question was asked the tourist guide had the amazing ability to completely ignore the individual.

One of our experiences included a visit into a small commune where, with great pride, one of the four families living in this small cement structure served us tea. This afternoon tea must have been very costly for the family who, clearly, lived a very Spartan life-style. In 1982, when we visited China, the government still stipu-lated that private enterprises of any description were not allowed. Therefore, farmers growing vegetables, for example, did not have an outlet for selling their produce. They had no source of income other than the government stipend. It gave me pause to compare our opulent lifestyle with that of the Chinese people at that time.

We were scheduled to fly out of Shanghai one morning at ten o'clock. At six thirty we were all awakened, told to quickly prepare ourselves because our travel plans had changed. As we were escorted out of the hotel, box lunches containing a breakfast of hard-boiled egg, an egg sandwich and an apple were thrust into our hands. The small plane didn't have enough seats to accommo-date all of us. So, nonchalantly as if it were a common occurrence, chairs were placed in the middle of the aisle! Why bother with seatbelts? Our company president, representing the multi-million dollar company, Aegon, found himself sitting on a folding chair in an airplane, without even a seat belt to secure him.

Other memories that float to the surface when thinking of our visit to China include seeing the negatives of pictures hanging on clothes lines; (presumably the negatives were viewed without being developed) and experiencing crowds of people wherever we found ourselves, with bicycles too numerous to count. In 1982 bikes were the only mode of transportation for all but a select few. Our tour guide informed us that the waiting time to be able to purchase a bike was at least two years; even with that restriction hundreds and hundreds of bikes filled the city parking lots.

TOKYO: In Japan, we were treated to a trip on Japan's famous bullet train where we were served tea as the train raced by Mount Fuji. It was apparently highly unusual to be able to see the mountain, most often it is hidden behind clouds. Leaning back on the lace covered seats, sipping tea, we became fast friends with John and Judy Kisellis from San Antonio; a relationship that continues today. Transamerica had a practice of passing out cash, giving all the attendees an opportunity to explore the local eateries for lunch. The stipend that time was $100.00 each to pay for a small salad. It certainly opened our eyes to the high cost of groceries beyond Canada. The Japan we saw was meticulous; white gloved chauffeurs dusting their vehicles, trees artistically pruned one tiny leaf at a time, streets continually being swept.

CANCUN: We were invited to swim in the warm waters of Cancun in Mexico at a time when the current Prime Minister, Pierre Trudeau, had just vacated our hotel. Our hotel was the typical clay adobe style, complete with tile floors but undrinkable water. A warning of Montezuma's revenge was the daily topic. Every morning we greeted the geckos who shared our room and realized their claim to the accommodations was a valid as ours. While in Mexico, a day long bus trip brought us to the historical Inca community of Cinchinitza. Ben, courage in hand, climbed the pyramids and then slid into the foundational tunnels. Claustrophobia and acrophobia have long been my companions; therefore, I became enchanted with a far corner of the gardens. I spent the time listening to the guide describing, in great detail, the varied methods of human sacrifices. I'm not sure which was more unsettling, the claustrophobic and acrophobia of the pyramids or the horror of the religious rites of that early civilization.

SYDNEY: Since my Uncle Gerhard and Aunt Audrey Baergen lived in Brisbane, Australia, it was very exciting to learn Ben had qualified for a conference in Sydney. After the conference in Sydney we spent time in Brisbane.

My Uncle and Aunt have lived in Brisbane since the end of World War II, after they were released from the internment camp where they were held as Japanese prisoners of war. For years they were the respite home for missionaries around the world. Being with them on the stunningly beautiful Gold Coast was an incredibly rich experience. I felt it was such a bonus to be able to hear how their love for God has expressed itself in the lives of those around them.

My uncle was an amazing personal tour guide. He made the sheep shearing demonstration, meeting the koala bears and the kangaroos, the colorful parrots, and the beautiful fruit gardens so much more meaningful than those experiences would have been for us as uninformed tourists

We were able to break up the long flight to Australia by spending time in Fiji as well as in Tahiti. There is certainly a relaxed flavor in those two islands with their blue waters, undulating waves, and long sunsets during which we shared in the tradition of ending the day enjoying the romantic tikka torches on the beach.

When in Tahiti we discovered a new way of dealing with the arrogance of some nationalities. Sitting down in the hotel restaurant, I noticed an appetizing fruit platter in the display case and asked the waitress for just that item. When my order came, the fruit was decidedly not fresh, so I asked the waitress to replace it with the one in the display case. She motioned that she could not understand English, only French; my plate was not exchanged. However, when the bill arrived, and Ben decided to add the food cost to the Hotel bill, she was able to tell us in perfect English that this was not an option; he had to pay the bill with her otherwise she wouldn't get her tip.

LISBON: Years later the Transamerica conference was in Lisbon, Portugal and we enjoyed a bus tour of that country. Again we found a certain familiarity, probably because of the historical faith connection in that part of Europe. Our tour guide was extraordinarily skilled, very well informed and quick to perceive which historical destination we might find interesting. We loved Portugal; the warmth we experienced from the Portuguese people was unparalleled. As we experienced their ceramic expertise, heard the stork stories, and saw the cork trees, we felt such a sense of community. It was decided that coming back to vacation again in the Algarve was going to be something we would file as a 'redo.'

WASHINGTON, DC: I remember the days spent in Washington, DC as the most informative and emotionally draining of our travel experiences. We were determined to soak up as much of the Smithsonian museums as possible, and came away totally exhausted. The images and displays in the Holocaust Memorial will always be burned into my brain. Atrocities have been experienced by many people groups in history. For example, I remembered the Armenian massacre in Turkey, the expunging of the nomadic Gypsies in Russia, and the displacement of Mennonite people in Ukraine. In Washington, the Jewish people have exposed their pain very dramatically; it's difficult to walk away unchanged.

The usual energy and pleasure of a fun vacation dissipated as I was confronted with the evil of man's inhumanity to man. The museum and the Holocaust memorial overwhelmed me; when power is abused the results are horrific. This tragic side by side positioning of human slaughter with the celebration of America's war victories overwhelmed me. Since America has been at war for more than half its existence, its history is a litany of one war after another. I found it to be very disturbing. The United States of America is indeed a warring nation.

Mennonites, my people, were birthed by a far deeper call, a call to pacifism. Being a pacifist is exactly that, being passive. I believe, however, our faith group is called to be active as reconcilers and peace makers. Peace keeping is noble, however, the higher call is to reconcile people groups, first to God and then to each other. This faith and tradition is my Mennonite heritage, it's where my theology and ethical posture was established.

The trip to Washington took my emotions in conflicting directions; the deeply disturbing political and historical exposure collided with the comforts of luxurious living, the enriching new geographical experiences, and the refreshment of time away. Reflection on these privileges drew me back to the blessing of privilege.

Growing up in the Rosemary farming community, I would never have dreamt I would relax in the Virgin Islands, be treated to the romantic luxury of Monaco, ski in Grey Rocks, Quebec, or watch the World Championship speed skating in Calgary. We were given tickets for the 1984 Olympics in Los Angeles. Ben and I have toured the world famous Carmel in California, played at Disney World in Orlando as well as Disneyland in Los Angeles where the parks were limited to Transamerica folks only.

The one country which treated us with disdain was Sweden. Their young people pontificated endlessly about their country's superiority and seemed to find it difficult to be gracious to these polite Canadian tourists. With that one exception, we experienced welcoming, engaging, and delightful people all over the globe.

Ben and I had our own version of 'Jeopardy' while watching the television program 'Lives of the Rich and Famous.' We had been privileged to be served in many of those luxury hotels and had tasted the lives of the rich ourselves. Amazingly, considering all the thousands of miles we have travelled, our luggage has always stayed on the journey with us, arriving not only at our destination intact, but returning home as well. God seems to have assigned special angelic beings to not only the two of us, but over our children as well when we left them with caregivers year after year.

The one anxiety which chronically revisited me from one year to the next was the trauma of entrusting the care of our sons to another person, sometimes for as long as three weeks. Most of those caregivers selflessly loved our boys; others did not. The cloak of regret for those experiences which were forced on them occasionally still clings to my shoulders. Those are experiences which I trust their Heavenly Father will heal and sort out in their psyches.

Many years earlier, in 1973, Ben presented me new set of luggage at Christmas. As he passed the suitcases over to me, he remarked "One day we're going to do a lot of traveling." Even though I was delighted with the gift, I found it hard to hide my skepticism. At that time, neither he nor I had any idea of what the future would hold; however, forty-one world destinations later his foresight has been proven.

In 2012, Ben made the decision to pull back somewhat from the constant pressure of selling; consequently we will no longer be treated to these international get-aways. I must say I am quite at rest about limiting our traveling. Airports are a huge source of frustration for me. Being the recipient of new hip joints seems to give officials endless permission to be groped. The bells begin to ring as soon as I cross into the security scanner and the disrobing begins: I know the drill.

The reflections of globe-trotting are inserted into this memoir only to offer another window into the extravagant blessings with which God has covered our lives.

20

THE BIRTHDAY PARTEE

I sat debating how best to celebrate my sixty-fifth Birthday. An idea slowly began taking shape as I threw questions into a brain which could very well be atrophied. I was searching for creativity. Did I want to commemorate becoming sixty-five privately, or not? How did I want to celebrate? Would I leave the planning up to my husband; to my sons or daughters-in-law? They had done a fabulous job of putting together my sixtieth celebration; surprising me with more than forty women, all dressed in hats and scarves, just as the invitation had directed 'come dressed as Edith would.'

An idea began to take shape. I would throw myself a surprise birthday party. At first blush that sounds like I had befriended dementia, or was anticipating not being able to hold one coherent thought in my brain when I turned sixty-five. That wasn't the case. I wanted to plan a party for the girls here in Williams Lake who were close to me. Those women, who regardless of age, were the ones who knew me best and with whom I had been able to walk with trust and deep affection; I wanted to express my gratitude for their friendship. At some time each had given me their love, each had spoken encouragement, and, at strategic times, had been the Voice of God to me.

Since I grew up in a family of boys, and then had three sons, girlfriends had always been very significant in my life. I had always envied those who had a sister. Working diligently at maintaining friendships I had tried to fill the empty 'sister' container.

My planning began to have substance. Using the surprise tactic came from my desire to circumvent the small town gossip of 'have you been invited to the party?' This was inordinately naïve thinking on my part, as it turned out. First a date needed to be chosen. The party needed to be far enough in advance of my birthday, or long after the April 13th date, thereby removing me from suspicion. Six weeks after I officially became a senior should be just about right.

Next the list of celebrants needed to be formed. I distilled the list down to sixteen. It has always been a deep conviction of mine that I should have friends ten years younger and ten years older than myself. So the guest list would include women in their third act of life, as I was; women in their second act, and even some under thirty years old.

Choosing a venue came next. Obviously the party could not be at my home. Someone needed to be invited in to the planning, someone who would be willing to divert conversation, even benignly outright lie, when questioned—and in the lie, be believable. They also needed to have a living room large enough to host such an event. Ah, I found just the right girl. Esther Corbett is a woman young enough to be my daughter who has become an intimate friend. Excitement bubbled in my thinking.

How could I maintain secrecy while getting the invitations delivered? The 'General Delivery" service of the local post office was just the avenue I needed. The fine gentlemen there joined in the spirit of the 'Partee' assuring me they would seamlessly ensure that I received all the returned envelopes. Personally addressed invitations were composed; lyrical and innocuous; giving no hint as to the reason for celebrating.

*A good friend of yours
is launching herself into
new territory; come be
part of the celebration.*

Only the date was added, indicating a response was mandatory. Each invitation carried the strict admonishment that the
celebration was a surprise and advising that when the sender
received the RSVP, further instructions would be given. Tucked
inside was stamped, self-addressed envelope to Partee, General
Delivery, Williams Lake. Eagerly I began checking the post office
as I waited for the responses to return. Three replies dribbled in.
WHAT? I was stunned, why would my friends not reply? I was
confused, then I realized they didn't know why they were being
invited, nor did they know to whom or to what they were agreeing.

My friends, I discovered, were inordinately suspicious.
Fragments of comments began to drift back to me, 'I'm NOT
replying to an unknown'…'It's probably one of those home
parties, I'm not being suckered into one of them again' I discovered that the very scenario I had hoped to avoid, that of gossip
comparisons, had found fertile ground with a large crop of gossip
ripening. Anxious conferences with my hostess friend ensued. A
second invitation was needed;

*Your Friend's a little worried
that you're not going to show.
It REALLY is a PARTEE.
She's not trying to steal your dough $$,
so find that invitation,
the one tossed in your trash.
Come prepared to have some fun;*
cause it's a BIRTHDAY BASH!!

And we waited again. This time all but three replied. We resorted to one more invite;

> *So very sorry*
> *you're not coming to the*
> *Birthday Bash.*
> *If you change your mind…*
> *remember, RSVP*
> *partee,*
> *General Delivery, Williams Lake*
> *No RSVP, No Final Instructions!!!*

Two more replies; one holdout. Finally I enlisted the help of my good friend Chris, one of those invited who would be on vacation and therefore unable to attend. She would make the phone call telling the one holdout that she would be oh, so very sorry if she chose not to attend. Chris explained that it was a legitimate celebration, not a sales party. We had manipulated, coerced, and lied, all in an effort to celebrate friendship.

The last invitation was sent:

> **PARTEE TIME**
> *May 24, 2008 7:30 pm*
> *So come to the House*
> *At the end at the Lake*
> *A family of Six*
> *And a Partee awaits*
> *Off to the left, next Right, and Right*
> *Then you're there!!*
> *Look for a Tall Man*
> *Who's got no Hair!*
> *The Name of the Road*

I'll give you a Clue
Think 'Derby' Think Horses
And think 'Grass That's Blue'
Confused?? Lost??
A Last Resort, A Phone Number
604-217-5393
On Saturday, not before
See you at the Door

Arriving at Esther's house in Lexington Subdivision along with the other invited guests, I too wondered out loud whom the party was for. "Me? No, not me, my birthday is long past, you know. 'Must be Shirley's; her birthday is right around now, isn't it?' We gathered and waited. Esther, ready with another ingenious plan, had prepared a word jumble/acrostic game to flush out the guilty party. The acrostic spelled 'she's got the laugh'…and so the party finally began.

I shared with the women that the evening was to honor my girlfriends. Each one had uniquely impacted my life; therefore the theme of the night was "let's celebrate friendships." In the past years there had been a time when each one had believed in me, had encouraged me to stretch and grow, had shared a pain, pushed me to laugh, or allowed me to be sad, all without recriminations. I wanted to acknowledge what each friend meant to me.

Over the weeks of preparation, I had asked the Lord to show me a specific encouragement from the Bible that would symbolize the uniqueness of each friend's contribution to my life. A few short, individual thoughts had been given to me. The evening was rich, emotional, full of laughter and, in my mind, clearly hit the mark. All the lies, all the subterfuge, were forgiven.

Toward the end of my planning I had invited Ang to work with me on the dessert, adding someone who was in their First Act of life to my basket of "sisters." With graciousness and decorum Ang hovered all evening, ensuring drinks and desserts were supplied. Kudos to Esther and Ang; I am indebted to them for their enthusiastic encouragement that ensured the evening will remain a bright light in my memories. The party was a highlight for me; the joy of reliving and retelling the story continues to increase the richness of my life.

21

THINGS I LEARNED FROM MY PARENTS

Pay close attention to what your father tells you;
never forget what you learned at your mother's knee.

~Proverbs 1:8~9

Two things are paramount: salvation through Jesus Christ, the Son of God,
and telling others about Him.

God is the Creator and Author of everything and everyone.

The Bible is my Guidebook; it is Truth, the inspired Word of God.
The stories really happened; treat every teaching in it as holy.

Prayer is always powerful.
God hears every prayer, spoken or unspoken.

Although I will never understand everything in the Bible,
I must choose to believe and live by its principles.

God is Sovereign and Trustworthy, God has a Plan for me.
God's ways are a mystery; trusting Him is imperative.

Faith must be learned and practiced.

Pride is an abomination to God, second only to Godlessness.

It's more important to honor your parents than love them.

Never be rude or use crude gestures or language.

Never expose your children's mistakes to others.

Always speak well of your spouse, especially to your children.
Never expose your spouse's shortcomings.

Avoid bragging, complaining, and gossiping.

Life is a very serious endeavor; shallow living is to be abhorred.

Always remember whose child you are.

Be sure your sins will find you out.

Life on earth is to be endured since we are only pilgrims
passing through this world; our real home is heaven.

Those around you in life are always watching, leave a positive imprint.

I am God's steward of all that I do, and all that I consume,
therefore waste nothing.

A life of wealth and luxurious living is ungodly and prideful.

Tithing is crucial in order to grow in the Lord.

Give thanks in everything for this is the Will of the Lord.

-January 24, 2005

22

ANGELS ON DUTY

Our first home in Williams Lake sat at the end of a long curved and climbing driveway that was approximately a city block long. There were no flat spots to grab traction on an icy winter afternoon. We were hidden by the hills to the southwest; on most winter days the sun would hit the driveway long enough to guarantee a wonderful skating surface going downhill; however, going uphill was another matter entirely.

As a farm girl I was used to driving trucks; so was usually quite confident maneuvering my way up the driveway, invariably with three little boys tucked into my 1965 Beaumont; trunk packed tightly with groceries. The car had two seatbelts in the front, none in the back.

On this particular day I was again in full 'Mom' mode, on my way home from the grocery store, and since it was around four pm, I was in a hurry to get home for the five pm suppertime. Seven year-old Chad was sitting beside me in the front seat, holding three month old Scottie in his lap; Kyle, five years old, was in the back seat. By late afternoon, the ice had comfortably settled on the tree-lined road and as, I rounded the first curve of our driveway, I realized, 'this is not going to go well today.' The second curve confirmed the Beaumont would not be successful in going up...so the car decided it would do the next best thing; slide back down.

In most cases, that wouldn't have been traumatic. Unfortunately, even for the most experienced driver, it's very difficult to keep a car sliding backwards, on a curved driveway, regardless of how well the tires hug the road. So what began as a gradual slide, very quickly became a hurtling accident waiting to happen. This would have been the time four angels, one for each of us, were called into action. Although the driveway began innocently, if one decided to be a bit adventuresome, or impatient to get to the main road, one could choose to make a leap over the fifteen-foot bank as a shortcut. It seemed that's exactly what the Beaumont decided would be the best route on this gray winter afternoon.

Years earlier, in anticipation of just such an event, the responsible people at BC Hydro had strategically planted a large hydro pole so it could benignly overlook the bank. It seemed that my car was determined to intimately greet this pole when, to our complete surprise, the car jerked to a sharp stop. I sat there, too dumbfounded to do or say anything for a minute. Gingerly opening the door and looking out, I realized that I had turned my front wheels to the right, so that with delicate precision those four angels had tucked the guy wire from the hydro pole in behind the wheel, in fact in the front wheel well of the driver's side of the car. Amazing.

A car with three grade twelve students pulled off the road and into the entrance of the driveway. The young men were concerned, "Is everything alright," they asked. I shrugged, oh so casually, and managed, "Everything's fine. Nothing to worry about."

Who but the Almighty could have engineered such a dramatic rescue? The Israelites, in another lifetime, were instructed time and time again to "build an altar"; do something to remind oneself of, yet another, miracle from the loving hand of the Heavenly Father. Our afternoon experience begged to be used as an object lesson to remind our small family: "And He shall give his Angels charge over you to guard you in all your ways."

GOD THOUGHTS

Reflections on journeying with God

God has reminded me time and again
of His words to the Roman society generations ago:
"For although they knew God, they neither glorified Him
as God nor gave thanks to Him."
There is an urge within me to give thanks and to record
the many times God has intervened in my life and in the lives of those I love.
Sadly, I have met only with moderate and intermittent success.
My 'Thanks, God' has too often been a thought
only in my spirit without pen ever touching paper.
The thoughts I write mentally,
although I visualize them in a brilliant red script;
are written with vanishing ink.
This is an undeniable truth in my life.
Frequently I have determined within myself to become a
prolific journalist; however, to my disappointment,
I have discovered a fickleness within myself that is difficult to conquer.
The few thoughts I have shared on the following pages
are insights God has been faithful to infuse into my spirit
on some of the those days when I have been successful
in quietening myself long enough to hear His voice.

23

THE GRACE OF GOD

Grace: The empowering Presence of God, enabling me to become all He's
Created for me to be and to do whatever God has purposed for me to do.
                                                                    –James Ryle

God's Grace is Promiscuous;
unrestrained, unstoppable; it has no fences, no boundaries;
nighttime doesn't deplete it,
year`s end doesn't terminate the journey.
There is no finish line.
searching, seeking, looking; it is by definition
Grace—God's Presence—and He will always come searching.

He walked through Galilee to find the woman caught in adultery.
He made the journey to find Zacchaeus;
Grace always comes looking.
He found Matthew, the tax collector.
He found Luke the doctor.
He found the fishermen.
He found the small boy with the loaves and fishes.
And He found me.

God's grace is without restraint;
God always comes looking.
No force can stand against Him
not addiction, not despair, not coldness:
not apathy, not weariness, not exhilaration
not doubt, not cynicism
not atheism, not agnosticism, not humanism
not culture, not status, not class systems,
not other religions, nothing will stop His Grace.

Grace, 'the Empowering Presence of Jesus'
always searching, looking for what and who is lost.
Grace, that Supernatural Force renewing my mind,
catapulting me into mental transformation
toward the place where
what is in my heart is a sweet aroma to God.

-July 2013

24

THE INNER GARDEN
Reflections Of A Sixty Year Old

My garden is hidden from the naked eye. Fruits struggle through unseen growth. Veiled too, are the flowers blooming in their season, how they flourish for a time; then replaced by others just as beautiful, just as fragrant. However, anyone who interacts with me reaps not only the tasty harvest, enjoys the perfumed flowers, but also the sour acerbic fruit that has ripened.

My garden is within; it's the garden of my soul, my inner thoughts, my private wrestling. Plant life reflects the hidden roots. So also my outward attitudes, my overt speech and actions are simply the result of self-talk and yes, the conversational prayer, the continuous murmurings of my mind.

At age thirty I became consciously aware of what was growing in my inner garden. In that season of my life the little phrase, 'as a man thinketh in his heart, so is he' grabbed my heart; then inserted itself into the regurgitations of self reflections.

It was not until then that I realized that a praiseworthy or honorable character was not a given; not something that happened automatically. I could, with selfish passiveness, allow countless negative habits and attitudes to flourish. Anyone within my company could be emotionally strengthened, motivated, or encouraged by what came out of my mouth. Or, conversely, their assessment could be "she stomped all over my garden with her big muddy boots."

Early in my self-analysis I realized I needed to be accountable for my speech patterns. I so hoped that the well-known idiom 'A word aptly spoken is like apples of gold in settings of silver' would accurately describe my conversations. There was always the choice between sweetness and sarcasm, encouragement or criticism, passive aggressiveness or truth spoken in love.

My internal, intimate speech patterns needed an overhaul. My criteria would be: how did I want to be defined by others, and how did I want to define myself. I knew I longed to be my own hero.

A sweet, juicy peach at its peak of ripe perfection makes the eyes glaze, the taste buds awaken and the mouth waters. Just so, I wanted those with whom I interacted to covet more of my friendship. I was very familiar with the bite of thoughtless observations as one more chunk of my self-worth disappeared. This world needs one less such pundit. The Holy Spirit needed to come; He needed to slice up my inner conversations so they could be nourishment. I wanted to be able to be the seamless channel so a Godly voice could be heard.

My conversations should not cause humiliation or the feeling of being diminished. The red flush, the tightly pursed lips, the downcast eyes, these were all reactions I knew well. They were all indications that the fruit of my garden was anything but palatable, certainly not delectable. Be aware and practice, be aware and be intentional became my mantra. I wanted my interactions to be such that it could be said of me "she walked through the daily intercourse of life without causing pain."

Selectively and purposefully I pursued positive input in my reading. I listened to the conversations around me; mentally highlighting phrases that I wanted to reuse, and just as quickly discarding those I wanted to avoid. Slowly a metamorphosis occurred in my *Welt Anschaung*, in my world view. Systematically I ploughed through judgmental, bitter roots.

Unknown to them, a handful of acquaintances, unknowingly, became my mentors as I fertilized, watered, and prayed over the soil in my garden. Flowers of acceptance, empathy, and understanding were coaxed along, fertilized by what I chose to listen to, chose to read, or use for reflection. Listening carefully to those I wanted to emulate I heard words chosen circumspectly, appropriately, and with forethought.

These many years later, how am I doing? Self-analysis announces that perhaps, to a small degree I have been successful in exchanging tart lemons for sweet strawberries, or have been able to pass on the sold nutrition of root vegetables. Every so often I will leave a conversation confident that something noble has passed between us. The residue left behind is the fragrance of beauty, there is a sense of having been an inspiration, or an encouragement to a fellow traveler. Truly, the journey of becoming is life-long.

> Let the words of my mouth and the meditation of
> my heart be acceptable in Your Sight, O Lord ~
>
> Psalm 19:14

25

A LASTING FRAGRANCE

For we are the Fragrance of Christ...

~2 Corinthians 2:15

It's the Christmas season. The votive candles are festively wrapped in a fabric gift bag; shining, bright red, appropriate for the season.

What is it about candles—from the outward appearance; the shapes are the same—as are we people. Candles come in so many, many colors, as individual as personalities. The uniqueness of each candle is in the fragrance. A new fragrance wafts the room as a votive is lit.

And so it is with us, we are really only fragrant when we are 'lit' with the Spirit of Jesus in us. The fragrance of the candle is a result of what has been mixed with wax, and so it is in each life.

The unique fragrance is a result of every experience we have walked through; the difficult and the delightful, the sour and the sweet; the painful and the exhilarating. We are distinctive because of our life in God; that is the individuality that shapes each of us.

Our exclusive 'Fragrance' is the expression of our faith, the result of the life we have, and are, living. No event in our life is without merit, every experience can be mined for profit; for the treasure God wants to give us after we have worked our way through.

The bouquet of the candle; the individual fragrance of the candle lingers in the room long after the light is extinguished. When the Spirit of the Living God rests in us, it is then that the impact transfers to all those in our circle.

The scent of peace and gentleness, kindness and empathy, forgiveness and compassion remain as a deposit of God. It surely leaves an aura, a fragrance hovering in the room, long after we are gone.

-December 2014

26

THOUGHTS ON 'THE LORD'S WILL'

...whenever you face trials of any kind, consider it pure joy, because you know that the testing of your faith produces endurance; and let endurance have its full effect, so that you may be mature and complete, lacking in nothing.

–James 1:2–4

I t's now my opinion that I have often misunderstand the larger scope of the Lord's will. We seem to have the understanding that when all goes well, our marriages work, our children grow up obedient, physically healthy, spiritually healthy, emotionally healthy, and the flow of finances doesn't put a cramp on the toys we want to buy, then we *must* be favored by God. And, if we and our children sit smugly in the front row at church every week, shouldn't the natural outcome be that our benevolent Heavenly Father smiles down on us while pouring out those lavish gifts on us; gifts we so richly deserve?

I no longer subscribe to that particular theology. I think God's purpose is to make us into " the chosen by God, chosen for the high calling of priestly work, chosen to be a holy people, God's instruments to do his work and speak out for him" as St. Peter writes so succinctly in 1 Peter 2:9. Being people, the only way we become who God has designed us to be, is through the challenges of daily life. This metamorphosis NEVER seems to happen when things go smoothly. Often I have chosen to ignore the little injunction "Consider it a sheer gift, friends, when tests and challenges come at you from all sides. You know that under pressure, your faith-life is forced into the open and shows its true colors. So don't try to get out of anything prematurely. Let it do its work so you become mature and well-developed, not deficient in any way." James 1:2-4.

Sometimes the bumps in the road are a result of my own profoundly silly decisions; other times I have reaped someone else's selfish choices. Still other times I can't pin the valley I'm in on anyone else, it's just life on planet earth. Thinking that a loving God owes me, or worse yet plans, a tranquil, idyllic lifestyle is such wrong thinking, in my view. Is it too strong a statement to comment that, as believers, we have at times misrepresented what picture Jesus painted of a Christ follower? We draw a rosy picture of our Heavenly Father, like Santa Claus, taking all our troubles, packing them up and as He takes charge of our lives, we live happily ever after. In my experience, life just never works that way. Our Kyle has said, "We just have to understand that life is hard, it just plain is. Why do we expect anything to go smoothly?"

Where I land spiritually and what has given me a great deal of peace is the sure knowledge that nothing happens in my life that has not first passed through the Hand of the Father where He gives it His stamp of approval. Is the difficulty I'm experiencing His purposeful design for me, or is He allowing it knowing that it has the potential of maturing me in Him? Compartmentalized in this way, I find life is so much easier to deal with. It seems to be my way of trusting in a good God who has promised He will always be totally aware of what is transpiring in my life

As I take a look back through the years, it seems many of Ben's and my challenging times of growth involved health issues. When Ben and I covenanted to marriage in 1967 we became one unit, therefore what one member of this unit experiences impacts the other as well. As far as I knew, I was completely healthy when, in 1989 I awoke on a Saturday morning from a good night's sleep with a high temperature and increasing back spasm. As the day progressed both symptoms became quite aggressive and demanded I be taken to the local hospital.

It would be four weeks in hospital, multiple blood tests, and x-rays not only here but also in Kamloops, BC. before the diagnosis of a staph infection resulting in septicemia was made. The bug had squirreled itself away hiding in my lower vertebrae. Following this diagnosis I was relegated to an additional four weeks flat on my back in hospital in the hope that the vertebrae, by now 'mush' from the infection, as my Doctor described it, would rejuvenate once the antibiotics had done their good work of killing the bug. Since much of my time during the first four weeks was spent enjoying the hallucinogenic properties of the medication used to mitigate my high temperature, Ben and my three sons bore the emotional brunt of my sickness. Each of them has a different view of that time.

My own memories of that time center on the tremendous gift the dear people from the community and particularly our church, were to us. Ben remembers, still with amazement, that during the nearly three months of my being in the hospital, he never had to cook an evening meal. Food arrived almost daily, and since it was November, December and January, our freezer was bursting with Christmas baking compliments of those who surrounded our family with their love. Numerous times I had angelic visitors at my side that would quietly encourage me, would read just one or two scripture verses, or would pray audibly for me. Although I have tended to be a voracious reader and one who loves to journal, I couldn't seem to manage either during those months. My Mom graciously came to shore up the male family for the last weeks of my hospital stay and the convalescing time at home.

Dr. Horace Willings, a profoundly spiritual English gentleman, who was known for his deep exegesis on scripture came to my bedside one morning and announced he had a word for me. In his heavily accented British he pontificated: "The Lord says to you, Edith, You will not die but live, and will proclaim what the Lord has done." (Psalm 118:17). Since my life at that point was indeed in jeopardy, I hugged his words tightly to my heart. Dr. Willings then plunked a massive blooming Amaryllis plant on my nightstand as a symbol of new life and disappeared.

I believe it was a point of contact for my faith; mentally I would say to God, 'Okay God, you promised.' Without a doubt I stumbled out of that valley far more certain that God was intrinsically aware of this child of His and that He could be trusted with my life.

Ben would say that dark season pushed him, a few months later, to a place of deep depression. His loving Father knew the dark abyss in Ben's psyche would need to be exposed at some point in his journey toward spiritual maturity; but at that time Ben had no grid for understanding depression. He unloaded to a dear friend and professional counselor, who recommended that he needed to have a clinical diagnosis. Medication was prescribed and during his healing time the Lord brought Ben to the place where he could examine his spiritual understanding of God. It became evident to him that God was asking him to come to a life stance of thankfulness. At first, strictly in obedience to what Ben saw as the quintessential teaching of Jesus, he began to say a blanket 'Thank you.' but without the joyful release that usually comes with genuine gratefulness. Next he began searching out scripture that dealt with the difficulties of life. He began writing out page after page of scripture in first person, declaring what God's promises were personally to him. The clouds began to lift only after Ben could authentically say, "Thank you Lord for exactly where I am today." He would daily continue to pray those personalized scriptures until they brought him to a new place in understanding of his good God. Emotional and mental healing followed.

The next challenge came when Ben returned from playing golf to discover that his elbow, which had felt a little tender when his game began, had swollen to the size of a small tennis ball. Having learned his lesson well from his brush with depression, Ben's instinctive response to the diagnosis of this being akin to the flesh eating disease was ' I will give thanks in all circumstances for this is God's will for "me." The elbow was incised and then was treated by daily debridement of dying tissue and, as antibiotics coursed into his veins, we continued to remind each other that God was totally aware and in control. From that perspective we could continue to give thanks. After a week of this regime and with no appreciable healing to be seen, our astute surgeon remarked that unless there was a dramatic change within twenty-four hours he would begin to enlarge the site and remove healthy tissue as well. He could see no other avenue to stop the continual dying of tissue. Our dear friends, the leaders of our local church body, surrounded us that night asking God on our behalf that He would be our great Physician that night and would begin healing. And God did. In the morning the change was remarkable. It was, once again, a faith building experience.

I've had a re-occurring dream for years and now I'm dreaming *again*, I'm bombing off a cliff, free-floating in thin air, unable to stop my downward spiral. I see the rocks grimacing up at me, and just before I greet them, I wake up. Co-incidentally, what should have been minor surgery in the summer of 1993, morphed into my nightmare becoming a reality. The anesthetic canister was inadvertently not refilled before the surgeon began his aggressive excision. Seething and scared out of my wits; all too aware of the scalpel's incision, I listened to the conversation between the surgeon and the anesthesiologist. "She'll be really glad she's having this done," one of them remarked. With eerie similarity to my recurring dream, I was impotent, I couldn't open my eyes; I couldn't yell or move. I would have liked to advise the team "hey, wait just one minute, I'm awake here, you know"—but I was mute.

I remember challenging God, wondering if He had forgotten to give my guardian angel instructions before He decided to have a quick snooze. I remember distinctly feeling really ticked off at God because I had asked Him to oversee what would be happening in the operating room that morning. From my perspective, that clearly was not the case. The anesthesiologist must somehow have been alerted that all was not well with his patient because my conscious mind next registered the warm voice of a very caring nurse coaxing me out of the anesthetic. Had I not had a clear memory of the conversation I heard, I would have surely thought it had been just another less than delightful 'pizza' dream. God has never explained Himself to me. I have to assume He knew there was something within my spiritual relationship with Him that would benefit from a severe, painful scare.

Other health issues came our way when I was first diagnosed with breast cancer and Ben with prostate cancer a year later. When the diagnosis of breast cancer came to me, I clearly heard God saying to me (in my head, not audibly) 'It's no big deal, honey, you'll be fine,' and I was. That doesn't mean God sovereignly zapped me and instantly the tumor disappeared. He used four weeks of radiation treatment in Vancouver to accomplish that so I could practice being thankful. I have no doubt it was His permissive will expressed in my life because He needed to shore up my faith in an area that I had not experienced being challenged.

While I was having radiation treatments in Vancouver I happened to see a documentary on various procedures to treat prostate cancer, profiling brachytherapy, which was the 'new kid on the block.' Ben and I chatted about the information and thought no more about it. A year later he was diagnosed with prostate cancer; it was immediately clear to both of us that God had prepared us a year earlier for this very event in regard to what procedure to choose. Brachytherapy was done on an outpatient basis, involving no surgery, and no chemotherapy. Side effects were purported to be minimal. Radiation pellets were inserted into the prostate to do the work of destroying the cancer. The procedure was a complete success and ten years later, Ben continues to have cancer-free checkups.

In both of visitations with cancer, we felt very covered with the cloak of God's love and a weird sense of peace that borders on denial. Because God created me and knows me intimately, He is also aware of what I need to experience next; to push me toward becoming mature spiritually. That's a soft and secure place for me to fall. I can rest there.

27

THE RAM IN THE THICKET

Before they call, I will answer. While they are still speaking I will hear.
~Isaiah 65:24

The surgeon is a young man, the shadow of teenage acne still on his face. He is not a day over thirty-five, I tell myself. This jock is going to define my life in the next few minutes. He plays volleyball with my son, for goodness sake. He's so self-assured; life really hasn't had time to sting him.

"So, as I suspected, the biopsy of your breast tissue did show a malignancy. Here's what I suggest we do."

We? Give me a chance to get in on your plan first, would you. How many times have you, just so casually, decided to mutilate that part of our anatomy which, I believe, physically defines me as being female.

'silence, I reminded myself.

I mean, you're nice enough, but this is my body you are about to abuse.

In my life God has not always allowed me to race around a problem on the 'Bypass Highway.' This was one of those times when I would have to go right through the city: long, slow red lights, stopping, starting, engine racing. I look at the change in the status of my health going from stellar to second-best as something to grieve but also as something God has entrusted to me. I believe that my walk through this experience will somehow highlight God's personal love for me. God is good all the time; I have not the slightest sliver of doubt that God loves me. His plan is for my good, I choose to believe Him when He tells me that. I am not the author of the cancer, which has decided to become intimate; and contrary to what some would have me believe, God is not punishing me for anything I have done. He has something wonderful in store for me. I think about what that might be.

When, like Abraham of old, I lay down my Isaac (that which I feel was a gift from God initially, like my health) without demanding that the thicket produce a ram, (without demanding that God take me *out* of the difficulty), only then do I find He is sufficient. In that place, with that mental stance, I can trust Him for what I cannot see.

The kind of faith God values seems to develop best when everything fuzzes over, when God stays silent, when the fog rolls in,

~Philip Yancey

Recently I was asked to pray for a woman who had just been diagnosed with breast cancer and was facing surgery. Desperate for hope she asked, "Did God reveal anything to you during your breast cancer experience that would help me?" Until she threw that question at me, I had not thought through God's response to my knee-jerk prayer at hearing my cancer diagnosis. In my spirit, though, I knew He had not brought me to a place where this cancer would threaten my life.

The incident became one of many I have experienced, where, before the question is fully formed in my brain, (it being marginally possible that I'm a little slow on the uptake) my Heavenly Father has already provided the answer. I have a God who daily intersects my life in marvelous ways. Unfortunately, most often I only recognize God's Hand in hindsight. In this spring of 2001, in this portion of my life's journey, there was a ram in my thicket. I was not asked to finish my life here on earth. Instead He gave me His sustaining umbrella of assurance that He was totally in control and that my health was His concern, His responsibility: there was no need for me to worry about it.

28

THE EMPTY TEMPLE

When the time comes for you to die, you need not be afraid,
because death cannot separate you from God's love.
                                                    ~Charles H. Spurgeon

The whisper of facial tissue, tears being stifled, the murmuring from the foyer, the funeral director soberly motioning people into the main sanctuary of the small Mennonite church in Prince George; these are the only breaks in the heavy silence. I'm at a funeral service for a young mother and her three children. My mind tells me this makes no sense, and I wonder where God is in this scenario.

By now the family of eight had planned to be settled among the First Nations people in northern BC. The father would have begun enthusiastically getting the family's life in order: planning the structure that would house his wife and six children, organizing the school courses the children would be taking under the dedicated teaching of his wife, organizing food stuffs which would need to be put aside for the winter's use and planning the first public gatherings where he could preach. It is the spring of 1976.

The young Mennonite family was in the process of moving from Oregon with a burning vision to share the Gospel of Jesus Christ to the First Nations people of northern British Columbia. Traveling north through the forests, fragrant with spring buds, they had been stopped by the rushing waters of an engorged creek. Together the adults, three teenagers and three pre-school children had prayed, asking the Lord for wisdom in their dilemma. They felt wisdom had been given; they would build a raft, which would safely carry all of them across the cold, racing water. It was not to be, as the raft began maneuvering through the rushing waters, the quickly built craft began to break apart. Of the family of eight only the three teenagers and their father survived.

Now, he stood behind the open casket facing the small grieving congregation in the Mennonite Brethren church in Prince George. His three teenage children stood somberly beside him. As her husband, he extended the invitation to view the lifeless body of his wife, the empty temple that had housed his life partner. As each person came forward for the viewing, he and his children greeted them. He seemed so composed, even on this--conceivably—the worst day of his life. Especially painful was the fact that the children's bodies had yet to be retrieved from the frigid waters of the swollen creek. However, he continued to lead the service with graciousness, sincerity, and with simple worship to God. It was reminiscent of Abraham those many generations ago when, just prior to offering up his son Isaac. Scripture records that Abraham was in the place of worship to his God in the face of, what he believed would be irreplaceable loss. The scene is also reminiscent of the Biblical Job, although the loss of his family was a part of the testing of God in his life.

Through the perspective of the elapsed years, I find that, not only do I not have answers for the questions which plagued me at that time; indeed new ones have climbed onto the pile, also without resolution. The parents of the young mother, how could they come to terms with this tragedy? As grandparents, their young grandchildren ripped from their arms of relationship here on earth, where had they landed emotionally, had they found peace…or did it elude them?

Did God give insight into what had transpired in the heavenlies during the time the young mother was struggling, not only for the lives of her little ones, but her own life in the cold spring run-off? Does God honor decisions made in utter sincerity, yet ignorance, by His children whose one desire is to serve Him? Could not He, who has all authority in Heaven and on Earth, have harnessed the raft so that it would not dissimilate? And in the end, when I confront the unexplainable, the un-answerable; I am left only with this:

Can anything ever separate us from Christ's love? Does it mean He no longer loves us if we have trouble or calamity? …or are threatened with death? No, despite all these things, nothing can separate us from the Love of God.
~Romans 8:35

29

THE MOUNTAIN OF THE LORD

> On the mountain of the Lord it will be provided.
> —Genesis 22:14

What an interesting little clause. The background scene is the rescue of Isaac from the hand of his father, Abraham. Abraham was determined to sacrifice his only son, because God had asked him to. Before he could murder his son, God Almighty stopped him and pointed out a substitute; a ram that was hiding in the bushes. Consequently after Abraham's allegiance to God had been tested, the Genesis account reports that Abraham named the place "On the mountain of the Lord it will be provided."(Gen 22:14) We know Him as Jehovah Jirah. But the connotation, I believe, is that as I worship the Lord, God will meet whatever needs I have so that His will and His Purposes can be accomplished in my life—and maybe the lives of others too. The Message translation of the Bible reads "On the mountain of the Lord, He sees to it."

The mountain is the place where I meet God, where I turn away from the things that surround me in this day to day existence. In my spirit I intentionally look away from anything that is visible. This is the time I focus only on Him and worship Him for who He is. It doesn't actually say Abraham worshipped God there, it says only that he was in the place of worship, on the mountain where God had brought him. The Bible references say it is the temple mount, the place of worship. So when Abraham was in the place of worship, the position of worship, the posture of obedience, it was there that God shared his plans for him. This was where God spoke intimately to Abraham and he heard the prophetic words for his future.

So, one wonders, why does God sometimes withhold revealing His purposes to us? God says clearly that it's His delight to reveal Himself, His plans, and His designs for us. In Amos 3:7 we read "Surely God does nothing without revealing His plan to his servants." I believe that the impediment to revelation is my readiness to hear God's plans, not God's willingness to reveal them to me. God always desires to communicate with us. I do not always live in a receptive spirit.

The consequences of my not hearing God or of hearing God, but then refusing to obey Him, are not small. My loving Father knows that about me. I need to be intentional about harnessing my thought processes; not allow my mind to wander, but discipline my spirit when I am in the place of worship. It is then that I am able to hear God speak. I must choose to be obedient in order to worship in spirit and in truth.

God, would you help me to understand what it means to be authentic in my worship of you, the Most High God. And, in my understanding, would you infuse my spirit with genuine worship of You. In my own strength I am undone, unable to give you the honor You deserve, unable to love You as I ought, unable to obey as I ought. I acknowledge that only your Presence surrounding me in the place where I intentionally choose to meet with you can put my heart aright.

30

COME BUILD AN ALTAR

...To this will I appeal, the years at the right hand of the most High. I will remember the deeds of the Lord, I will remember your miracles of long ago. I will meditate on all your works and consider all your mighty deeds.

–Psalm 77:10–12

God often told the Israelites to build an altar, a place of remembrance when He had, yet again, rescued them. He knew that they were a people who were extremely forgetful and unthankful; unless they had a visual reminder they would never assimilate God's instruction about his love for them and that He is faithful to hear their cry for help. These many generations later, we really have not changed a lot.

When God brought the Jewish people through the Red Sea, when Jacob wrestled with the angel in the night, when God provided food in the wilderness He would then remind them, "build an altar so that when the tough times come in the future, you'll have a place to go where you can remember My faithfulness." I am so glad He insisted they remember His goodness, visually; it's a good reminder for me in the twenty-first century.

We are a fickle creation; we are not automatically a faith filled people who see our lives realistically. It is only with intention that I choose to view life through the lens of 'how has God intersected my life today to cover me with good?' As morning breaks apart the grey still clinging to the night, it is imperative that I breathe in faith and say 'the challenge of today is handed to me on a silver platter directly from the Almighty.' It's so easy for me to glibly live life with an assumption that I'm in control of daily events.

When I get discouraged, frustrated with the lack of change I see in myself (and others), I will remind myself of Your track record, Lord. I will remind myself of Your faithfulness to me year in, year out; and your faithfulness to all those who know You. I will remember the altars I have built in the past, the written memoirs describing the amazing way You have led; Your Presence is always closer than the air I breathe."

Remind me, Lord, and open my eyes to see the many times you have been faithful when I was unaware. I have certainly not given You the credit for your imprint on my life, for your maneuvering situations and people on my behalf. Behind the scenes, You have given health, wisdom, insight, and strategies; sadly, much too often without my acknowledgement. All I have and all that I am has been a gift to me.

As I intentionally choose to remember; Lord, please give me supernatural insight, showing me who You have been to me in my life. I don't want to become lazy in giving You credit for who You have been to my forefathers, who You are to my family and to me personally. You warned the Romans in their day that the debauchery which defined their society was the cause of an ungrateful, narcissistic, and selfish lifestyle. The thin line between their lifestyle and ours trembles. For the sake of the longevity of the society in which I live, Lord, would you work in me a generous and grateful heart.

-March 26, 2005

31

DINING BEFORE MY ENEMIES

You serve me a six course dinner right in front of my enemies.
~Psalm 23:5

I have a mental picture of a large, beautifully laid banquet table.
As I`m seated at the table, Jesus comes to serve me dinner.
Plates of food fill His arms, ready to be served one at a time.
I look around and I see shapes lurking around the edges of the table
my enemies; fear, confusion, depression, jealousy, untruthfulness,
laziness, pride, guilt, all are leering around the periphery,
sly, sneaky, disguised, evil personified.

As I sit expectantly
Jesus places the first course in front of me
a large platter of
courage,
looks like roast beef to me, good protein.
He whispers, eat this for your journey.
It will give you the stamina for what lies ahead.
He reminds me that I can do all things through Christ
who strengthens me.

He hands me a sliced-loaf of
right thinking
expressed through tactful speech.
I have to chew on that, eat it slowly and thoughtfully.
God has said I have the mind of Christ.
Therefore whenever I need wisdom,
He will speak wisdom into my heart,
and use me as His channel to love another
to encourage someone else.

Then He serves me some
contentment
It`s not hard to recognize those glistening barbequed spareribs,
meat falling off the bones, now those call contentment from far off!
He has said that through Him,
I can learn to be content in whatever state I am, it's a promise.
And He would remind me that He knows just what's best for me,
he'll always give me exactly that; He's always good.

Then He would pass me some
joy,
bright red and sparkling in a huge bowl.
I take big spoons full of that because
the joy of the Lord is my Strength;
it's not just an empty feeling of exhilaration,
but it is a state of being that is certain.
It fills me with hope for each new day,
and it strengthens me for lies ahead.
It's based on fact; He is my Rock and my Fortress.

Then I see him passing me a plate of
discipline
It`s a salad of raw vegetables, crunchy, chewable greens;
eat slowly, I tell myself
and He would remind me that whatever lack I feel,
He's equal to walking me through each discipline
that I can overcome any weakness I have in myself.
We walk shoulder to shoulder to give me confidence
the plate of discipline is a deep, strong dark blue.

Then Jesus comes close, puts an arm around my shoulder,
draws my head close to him as he holds a bowl of
comfort
for me to consume.
Eat it slowly, He says, taste it as it slips down your throat,
let it fill all the aching parts of your being.
I close my eyes and taste the nostalgic flavor
of my Mom's green bean soup.
Jesus, how did you know about those
hidden, aching muscles
the dried up dreams, the forgotten longings.

So very close to Him, He reminds me what he said centuries ago,
come to me all of you who are weary, tired,
weighed down with grief and loss.
Give me that heavy load you're carrying,
let me carry it for you
and I will give you rest from your grief.

And the last course, dessert certainly
it`s my favorite chocolate, pecan truffle cheesecake
with whipping cream, cherries and caramel sauce
surely guilt inducing, but Jesus calls it
freedom
As He slides an enormous piece onto my plate
He reminds me,
"There is now no condemnation for those who are in Christ Jesus."
My enemies would love to heap on the
'should haves, the could haves, and the would haves'
but I don't need to consume any of that,
I am free to be exactly who He designed me to be
free to laugh, skip with joy, and free to rest.

I have been served a gourmet feast,
a six course dinner, served on heavy white linen,
gold platters, shiny sterling silver ware, transparent crystal
free to be exactly who He designed me to be
free to laugh, skip with joy, and free to rest.

Dining in the presence of my enemies with Jesus as the Host,
passing the food just when I need it;
it's a rich, fulfilling life-style

I bask in His goodness, His lavishness
and the completeness of His banquet.
Remind me Lord, your banquet table is always ready.

-January 20, 2004

32

HEARING THE SHEPHERD

The sheep listen to His voice. They will never follow a stranger, in fact, they will run away from him because they do not recognize a stranger's voice.

~John 10:3, 5

The Voice calls His sheep by name, it is not addressing "Ladies and Gentlemen": it's intimate, it's personal, it singles me out from the crowd of life. His voice zeros in on me and calls me by my own personal name. It's never loud, clanging, or harsh; He speaks distinctively, clearly and very specifically.

His sheep are accustomed to Him speaking. When the Shepherd speaks, they're already listening with expectation. His sheep are anticipating His Voice. They are accustomed to listening for the message, knowing it will apply to them. As I wait for Flight 999 in the airport, for example, I tune my hearing for the expected flight announcement. I mentally sort and discard all other messages. Just so; the sheep are accustomed to listening for the message from *their* Shepherd, waiting for His personal instructions.

The Voice is pleasurable, it's welcome. There need be no fear, no apprehension in responding. It rises above the cacophony of all the other voices that insist on being heard, voices that jostle around for position in our head. His Voice stands distinctively apart. The Shepherd always gives positive instruction, encouragement, something applicable. These are the thoughts He drops into my soul; clearly, when I'm listening, my Shepherd will always make sure I Him.

"Today, I am your great I AM, whatever you have need of, I AM"
—Exodus 3:14

"Come to me. Get away with Me and you'll recover your life. Keep company with me and you'll learn to live freely and lightly"
—Matthew 11:28–29

"I'd never forget you, never. Look, I've written your name on the back of my hands."
—Isaiah 49:16

33

WHEN I THINK I'M GOING UNDER

When I think I'm going under, part the waters, Lord
When I see the waves around me, calm the sea
When I cry for help, Oh hear me Lord and hold out Your Hand
Touch my life, and still the raging storm in me.

My child, let me encourage you with Deuteronomy 7: 17-24 and in particular 7:22 and 23. "Do not be terrified by them (the things you now fear). The Lord your God will drive out these nations before you little by little. You will not be allowed to eliminate them all at once, or the wild animals will multiply around you. But the Lord your God will deliver them over to you throwing them into great confusion until they are destroyed."

We know the nations in the life of the Israelites are pictures of the things we struggle with in our walk toward maturity. Two examples of this imagery are, Canaanites as depictions 'depression or enslavement,' Hittites being defined as 'the fear of man.'

Terror, the kind that plunges your stomach down, and then knots it up tight is something we're familiar with, and it's my response to a situation over which I feel I have no control. It happens in the split second between the time I get bad news and the time I give it back to God for Him to defeat. Just as Israel was given a promise of accomplishing great things for and with God when they arrived in Canaan, ours is a promise of what God wants to do in our lives. And, similarly, the accomplishment of His promise is dependent on overcoming the enemies in our lives. How does that happen? It happens one situation at a time, one challenge at a time, and one day at a time. Having success in defeating an issue can come only by the infusion of His empower-ment. He won't do it all at once, the enemies have to be defeated one at a time, one challenge at a time; but He has promised, He will defeat them through us. It's been my experience He defeats the enslavement (or fear) one day at a time, one challenge at a time. We cannot 'white knuckle ourselves' into success by becom-ing mature overnight; that battle can only be won by giving God the opportunity to do it in us.

And, the good news is, we, your parents, are the fortunate ones as we watch you succeed in climbing this present mountain, the current dilemma. You have the God who has already decided you *will* win against this seemingly impossible mountain.

34

EMOTIONAL BONDAGE

Why are you downcast, O my soul? Why so disturbed within me? Put your hope in God, for I will yet praise him, My Savior and My God.
~Psalms 43:5

I need to be reminded of this verse when I need verification that my emotions need not control me. "I couldn't help myself;" "I can't help the way I feel;" "whenever this happens, I get so depressed;" "God gave me these desires, why shouldn't I act on them." It's difficult to take control over our feelings so they don't victimize us.

My emotional temperature rising, one of my sons once heard me remark, "I'm about to lose my victory"; he has lobbed it back to me whenever he feels my emotional temperature rising. Another son resorted to "hey, Mother, how's the air up there sitting on your high horse." We hear those comments so often, and always with the underlying understanding that our feelings have a right to control our lives. Can we really not help how we feel, are we really at the mercy of every emotional wave that attacks us, every desire that calls out to us?

When he wrote the Psalms, David made it very clear that he, cognitively, was taking control of his emotions. He stands back and says, "hey, soul (*mind, will & emotions*) what's the matter with you, why are you so depressed. I won't stand for it. You go ahead and be downcast; I, in my conscious, thinking self, I am not going to give in to depression. I am going to praise God, He's my Savior; He redeems my life, my every situation. I will not give in to being discouraged."

It certainly gives validity to the idea of writing out Psalms. When I have intentionally paraphrased the Psalms, writing them long hand, the words become life to me. This physical action somehow makes it's easier to hear God speak to me and for me to really hear Him so that it impacts my life to bring about change.

Clearly, this is not speaking of clinical depression, where medication is indicated. This is speaking of the 'poor me' attitude, the glass that is always almost empty attitude. God has meant for me to be an over-comer, one who 'reigns in life,' one who chooses to be 'on top of the heap.' Here is verification that self-talk is God ordained! I *can* talk myself into a change of attitude because it has God's stamp of approval all over it—and why? Because the thoughts that are changing my attitude are not just self-motivational thoughts, they are alive; they are supernaturally God-breathed. When I speak His truth to my soul, it becomes life, it has supernatural unction, supernatural energy.

Would you remind me, God, just as the poet David discovered, my emotions need not control me. All of the resources I need to commandeer my feelings are available to me through my Heavenly Father. God, You are my Source, You are my Rock, You are my Deliverer, You are my hiding Place, You are my Wisdom, You are my way through. ***You are my Joy.***

-January 13, 2005

35

ANNA'S STORY

Preface to Anna's Story

From my earliest remembrance I had assimilated strong beliefs about my faith, and had taken the stance that as Mennonites, as Christians, we were strangers here, exiles, refugees, and oddities. We were just passing through; our focus was always directed toward our eternal home. Many of the lyrics of traditional Mennonite songs embody a longing for heaven, and our ethnic melodies often are quite melancholy. Coupled with that theology, was the umbrella teaching of a *Lieber Heiland* and *Lieber Vater in dem Himmel* (loving Savior and our loving Father in Heaven). The compassionate love and faithfulness of our Father in Heaven and the efficacy of the death of Jesus on the Cross was foundational to all other theology. Also, it was a given that we could not understand the ways of God, we could not understand the why's of suffering, we could not understand the why's of the displacement of the Mennonite people generation after generation. But, even in that mystery, there was a sureness that God was faithful and His way was best.

I have memories of lying in bed during my childhood, over-hearing conversations describing the atrocities of the Communist regime in the Soviet Union, the evilness of Stalin, the indescrib-able horror that those believers who were left behind in the "old country" had to endure: the work camps in the freezing hell of Siberia and/or enduring every inhumanity and torture available to the known world at that time.

My father alone among his family was allowed to leave Russia; consequently no other male members survived the Communist purging. All of my mother's family members were allowed to leave, with the exception of my eldest Aunt, Marie, who had established her own family. Aunt Marie's husband was murdered shortly after the rest of her family had immigrated to Canada. It is from that backdrop that I have written the following short story with my mother as the main character. My desire is to honor those faith-ful, God-fearing people who have gone before me, leaving me an undeserved heritage: belief in the promises of God regardless of one's circumstances.

I have taken some literary latitude in some of the descriptions, however, the actual events are not fabricated, they are an accumu-lation of my own parents' and also my mother-in-law's autobio-graphical experiences, stories overheard and read. As well, I have availed myself of the work of Mennonite historians who faithfully documented facts, experiences and scenarios from the early years of the Mennonites who immigrated to Canada in the mid 1920's; experiences very similar to those of my own parents.

ANNA'S STORY

Anna Adrian

"All these people died still believing what God had promised them. They did not receive what was promised, but they saw it all from a distance and welcomed it. They agreed that they were foreigners and nomads here on earth. Obviously people who say such things are looking forward to a country they can call their own. If they longed for the country they came from, they could have gone back. But they were looking forward to a better place; a heavenly homeland." Hebrews 11:13-16

It was 1925; the harvest fields surrounding the little settlement in the Ukraine were silent. They were stripped and depleted. Even the low-hanging clouds in the motionless fall air looked melancholy. Twenty-two year old Anna stood looking out at the acres of desolation. Yesterday she had walked through the rows of harvested wheat for the last time. Her job had been to look for left over stalks of grain, little heads of wheat that could be carefully garnered, laid in a bucket, every kernel considered. Each kernel meant a little more porridge, or added to the few handfuls hoarded, it could mean one more loaf of bread.

Anna was tired. It was exhausting to be the third daughter of a farmer who longed for sons; to continually search for ways to assuage the guilt she felt at being yet another girl. So she continually worked harder in the fields, strengthening her muscles so she would be strong enough to work the long hours, to do the heavy lifting that would make her father proud of her. But her father longed for sons, sons who would help carry the burden of farm work. And now, after years of an enforced famine orchestrated by the new regime, an edict had come yesterday demanding everyone leave their farms within twenty-four hours.

"Anna," her mother called "stop daydreaming and help with the packing." Anna turned quickly, feeling guilty again, and bent her arms around the bedding, quickly scooping it up into a large fabric sack. "Mutti," she said, "Are you sure Grozmama and Grozpapa know we're going to be coming to stay with them?" Will they like us (her mind quickly added, 'will they like me'?) Anna couldn't remember her Grandparents; she had been only four when she had last seen them.

"No time to think about that now, Anna, we have no choice but to go to the Terek where we'll be safe for a while" her mother remarked tersely. "Did you say it would take us three days to get there?" "Yes, that is, if the weather stays the way it is now, but if it starts to snow"; her mother shrugged, "who knows how long it will take us if the weather turns? October can always bring snow."

If only the bandits hadn't come through the little village the week before and taken all the horses, traveling would have been so much easier, she thought. Life had seemed so much safer a year ago. But in the last months, nothing was secure and no one was safe. The forest surrounding the settlement was home to the notorious Machnov terrorists. Night after night they rode through the empty village streets, breaking into homes, stealing, looting, leaving many buildings in flames, and even kidnapping the young men. Anna was relieved that they would be getting away from the bandits, especially after yesterday....

The horror of the night before would not leave her today. She would never forget last evening as long as she lived, she was sure of it. Wednesday night was Youth night at the church. It was the highlight of the week; Anna and her friend Katie had not missed one gathering since they had reached the legitimate age of fifteen. After the meeting, they ambled slowly home. Rounding the corner from where they could see Katie's house, Katie exclaimed, "Oh, no, look at the horses outside my house." Anna saw immediately why there was such fear in Katie's voice...the horses were not from the village and she knew instinctively the Machnov bandits were once again in the village. Katie grabbed Anna's hand and held on so tightly, Anna winced in pain. "Don't let them see us," Anna whispered, her voice catching in her throat. Stealthily the two girls crept toward the back of the house. They heard shouting inside although they were not yet close to the house. The girls looked at each other, frozen in fear. Then they inched closer. Slowly, slowly, until they were right up against the back wall and just to the right was a window. Katie and Anna stood on tiptoes and inched their way up to peer inside. Too late the girls wished they weren't at the window. Anna would never forget the gruesome scene before her, Katie's father standing against one wall, arms raised in surrender, four men in torn, dirty, uniforms surrounding him in a half circle. A shot rang out and Katie's father slumped to the floor. The four men standing in the kitchen laughed raucously; one of them grabbed a saber and with one vicious swipe cut the throat of the dying man. Fainting, Katie slid down to the ground. Anna dropped down beside her, covering her friend with her arms and biting her lips to keep from screaming in terror. She heard the men, still laughing drunkenly, leave the house, climb onto their horses and ride out of the Village. Anna waited in silence, then Katie regained consciousness and together the two girls stumbled to Anna's house where they found Katie's mother sobbing in terror and anger. Katie blurted out that she had seen the Machnov bandits shoot her father just before another black curtain covered her and she fainted.

Now Anna shuddered--remembering—and quickly sorted clothes into small piles. Only the bare necessities would make the trip with them. They only had one wagon; she and her father would pull it together. She couldn't allow her mind to dwell on the two beautiful horses that she would no longer greet in the mornings. Briefly, she prayed, "Dear God, please let them be kind to our horses, they deserve to be treated well."

Late into the night the family sorted their belongings, debating over what they would need on the trip and choosing what would be packed in the wagon, and where the younger children would travel. Then came the discussion about the food; all that was left was a small sack of grain, another sack filled with roasted "zwieback" and a small stash of potatoes which they secreted into a hole dug in the dirt floor of the barn, disguised under sand and straw.

Although it was late and they all needed to get a few hours of sleep before the long journey the next day, Anna decided she would quickly go dig up the potatoes and put them into a sack ready for first light tomorrow. With quick precise movements she lit a lantern and made her way out to the barn. She opened the door; stepped back, startled. There in front of her were two men, dirty, disheveled, looking almost feral.

She stammered, "What are you doing here?" Before the words were out of her mouth, one of them sneered, "You think you're the only one who knew about your potatoes?" Their pockets bulged and their hands were full of potatoes. The hole was empty. There would be no potatoes to take along their journey. "Give them back...we need them, they're all we've got for three days of travel, please." They laughed at her, "You go tell your Papa that Yuri and Stefan came to collect payment for working on his farm last year."

She stumbled back to the house, her breath coming in ragged sobs. She could hardly get the words out as she tried to explain to Papa what had happened. She watched the emotions run across his face, anger; fear and then, once more she saw the all too familiar look of defeat as his shoulders slumped and he turned toward the bedroom. "God in heaven help us, what will become of us now" and then straightening, "Come, children, let's join hands and have the *Abend Segen*, (Evening blessing). "Our dear Heavenly Father," her father began slowly "as we lie down to rest this night, we thank you for your great love for us, for how you have blest us, thank you for the gift of your Son Jesus who died for us. We pray your comfort on our many brothers and sisters who have had such great losses. We thank you that you never slumber nor sleep and ask for your protection over our home this night. Amen." "Go to bed now, Anna; tomorrow we have a long journey."

It was in fact four long days before they arrived at her grandparents' home. At first Anna succumbed to her suffocating shyness. She hated it so, but she could hardly force a few words out of her mouth. By the next morning Anna felt a little more secure having lain in bed awake for a long time, mentally listing all the expressions of warmth she had felt from her grandparents. Then, as was her habit before she fell asleep, she had spent a few minutes having a silent conversation with her Heavenly Father, a conversation never limited by her shyness.

At the breakfast table, over steaming bowls of oatmeal, she listened with intense interest as the conversation revolved around the economic situation in Russia. Her grandfather had a deep rumbling authoritative voice "If the government hadn't demanded so much of our harvest last year, we would have been able to have some seed wheat. As it was we only had enough seed to pay what they wanted from our crop this year. That's why all our people are starving." More discussion followed.

Then father spoke up, "But Grandfather, tell me what is this we've heard about being able to emigrate to Canada. Mr. Wiebe says that the Canadian Pacific Railway, the CPR, will lend Mennonites the money to emigrate."

"Yes, Mr. Janz has been pleading with the Russian Government to let our people go. Sometimes it sounds like it's going to happen and then at the last minute, they change their minds." The talk went on late into the night. Anna heard names she would hear over and over in the next weeks; Colonel Dennis and Sir Edward Beatty. These two men, it seemed, were determined to persuade the Canadian government to allow a mass immigration from the Soviet Union and were tirelessly lobbying with the top Canadian officials.

"Father," Anna asked as soon as she found her father alone, "why would these two English men be speaking for us to the Canadian government." "Anna, I don't know, it seems as if God has inspired them, it could not be otherwise," he replied. "And there's another man, David Toews, who's already living in Canada; God is using him too. They have been sending delegations to the Government, pleading on our behalf."

'How very strange' thought Anna. Without even realizing what was happening, Anna's belief in the faithfulness of God was strengthened. If He would work in the minds of men who would aggressively lobby for her people, well, He could do anything.

"But, Father, none of us have any money. Two years ago we could have paid our own way, but everything has been taken from us, how will we ever be able to emigrate without any money?"

"Anna, I have no idea, we have to learn to trust in the goodness of God," he replied.

Years later Anna would read of the compassion and resolute doggedness of the men they had talked about that evening. She would read of the faith the two CPR executives had in a people unknown to them. Tenaciously, again and again, they petitioned the Canadian officials, begging them to act in a manner counter to the culture of the day and allow the Europeans to immigrate. Prejudice against anyone not Anglo Saxon infused the halls of Parliament. She would read that the CPR extended credit to an organization not yet established (the Mennonite Church of Canada). The credit, equivalent to ten million dollars was extended to twenty thousand destitute people who had no means to repay that debt. Colonel Dennis and Sir Edward Beatty staked their own resources, particularly their reputations, to rescue a people they did not know.

Reading this many years later, Anna reflected, "yes, but for the intensely committed leadership of those few men I would very likely be living—or most probably dead—in the former Soviet Union." These newcomers were wholly dependent on the favor of God as well as the benevolence of those Mennonites who had already settled in Canada. Although twenty thousand Mennonites were rescued at that time, another eighty thousand were tragically left behind when the Russian Iron Curtain slammed down in 1930.

The day after Anna and her family arrived at the home of her grandparents, her father applied to immigrate to Canada. It would be a year before all the travel documents for the family arrived; a year before the arrival of the chartered ships from Canada, before all the medical exams were passed, and the trains finally arrived at the little village station. The train would be full; the little station was packed with those leaving and those unable to leave. The mood was very somber. Each knew the finality of the goodbyes. Anna would remember her grandparents fighting to control their grief as they prayed God's blessing and protection on their children and grandchildren they were never to see again. Even the very stoic could not contain their tears or the occasional stifled sob.

Then a clear, firm male voice began singing, *God Be with You till we Meet Again.* Everyone, young and old, joined in as the blanket of God's powerful peace settled over His homeless children. Then the large red steam engine spewed and the train pulled away into the unknown.

On the ocean liner, seasickness defined Anna's days. Finally, early one morning on the ninth day, her father opened the door of the little cabin she shared with her three little brothers, and said "Anna, come quick, we're here, CANADA." Then the family rode another train: across Quebec, across Ontario, across Manitoba, and across Saskatchewan. For days she saw only miles of unending nothingness; and then finally, Alberta. Her seven thousand mile immigration had come to an end.

Anna had never seen so many people. They had come from all around the small Alberta community. One train after another pulled into the station and quickly disgorged its passengers. The newcomers stood bewildered. And then, slowly a deep bass voice began to sing and, as if gathered by a magnet, the crowd joined in singing "Praise God from Whom all Blessings Flow." When the anthem began, every male removed his hat in tribute to God. The significance of the song was not lost on anyone as grown men, young and old, struggled to hold back the emotion.

Within a week of arriving in the strangely welcoming land, Anna's parents moved into an abandoned farmhouse and Anna was offered a job as a live-in housekeeper. This would mean leaving her parental home for the first time. Demand for young women like Anna was fierce, they had become known for their diligence as well as their party-free lifestyle. Fear filled her but she knew she had no choice. She was the eldest; it was her responsibility to help sustain the family. Fear seemed to fill her very essence. "But father, how can I talk to this lady when I don't understand any English? And how can I cook when I don't know how to read English?" She wondered. Her father glanced at her with deep affection. How he loved this daughter and how he longed to be able to so provide for his family that there would be no need to depend on the income his children would bring. "Anna, you know God is faithful. I don't know how else to help you except to tell you I promise to pray for you every day"

But, sitting in the borrowed wagon, pulled by unfamiliar horses, Anna's apprehension only increased during the twenty-mile ride. She would be wholly dependent on the kindness and patience of Mrs. Proudfoot, her new employer.

In those first weeks, because of her acute shyness and now loneliness, Anna found the days unbearably long. Later she wrote in her diary that often sleep would only come after many tears. As the days slipped by, however, Anna found consistent kindness oozing from Mrs. Proudfoot. She was untiring in her willingness to teach Anna conversational English. She gently encouraged her daily to read new recipes, consequently Anna found herself becoming more and more confident. She was so thankful for her job; for many months the only income her parents had was what Anna would bring home. She was allowed one weekend a month to go home, but often needing her salary sooner, her father would drive to her workplace. There were four small children still at home needing to be fed.

In the following two years, Anna attended the Mennonite church in Tofield, Alberta and became casually acquainted with a young man, Leonard Adrian. One day Anna received a note. Leonard Adrian asked if he could see her on Sunday afternoon. Her heart pounded so fiercely she could hardly breathe. "Help me Father," she prayed, "What should I do." Instantly she heard the whisper of God, "This is a good man; he is My will for you." Anna took a deep breath and resolutely pushed all her misgivings into a far corner of her mind. She would not entertain them and before she could change her mind, she quickly responded with a one word "yes."

Marriage followed within a few months, then a move to another abandoned farmhouse. It was to be a year later before Anna and Leonard Adrian realized they had settled in an arid, unforgiving land, which harshly withheld fertility. It would demand backbreaking labor but would not respond with prosperity. Instead, with great effort, with emotional and physical pain, would they carve out an existence for their family during the ensuing twenty-five years. Three healthy children were born, three sons and then a daughter. The daily drudgery of eking out a living was overshadowed by the fulfillment Anna felt in her relationship with her Heavenly Father, the companionship and love of her husband, and the delight of raising her children. At last she had found why she existed. It was to join with her husband in forming a family under the umbrella of the guidance of God. Inhibited and withdrawn, she infused her family with her deep faith. She would not allow the poverty she felt in her relationships, the poverty she felt financially, nor the poverty of her words block her belief in or her communion with a loving heavenly Father. She saw only faithfulness and consistency in her conversations with God. At home, with the walls of the little farmhouse wrapped around her, her spirit expanded as she lavished love upon her family. Despite the unremitting challenge of providing even the most basic needs, she would later recount in her biography that her consuming joy was in the goodness of God who never disappointed her. As the children grew older she was often amazed at the wisdom she articulated, knowing it was supernatural, coming from beyond her.

Regularly, however, she continued to hear of horrors in Stalin's Russia as the very occasional letter would pass unnoticed through the labyrinth of inspections. Her dear friend, Lizzie Penner, in cryptic code told of escaping the shooting rampage of the bandits that killed her brother and ended in the burning of all the family owned. With each new disclosure, Anna's comprehension of God's amazing guidance and benevolence in her life increased.

The years fled by on slippered feet and Anna was now 90 years old. Her warm smile was still inviting, her blue eyes still glistened; she was still quick to grasp the humor in a comment. The autobiography which lay before her was almost finished. Her children and grandchildren needed to see life from her perspective. Carefully she wrote, "I recall the prayers I've prayed and the wonderful way God has answered. My family, my children have always had first place in my prayers. My prayer has always been that they would love the Lord, and serve him loyally." She sat back and thought about her loving husband whose death at age sixty-seven had left her unprepared for yet another dramatic new phase of life.

Leaning forward she mused "For me, Leonard's death was too soon, he was too young. But God in His wisdom called His child home and I submit to that." She put down her pen. Folding her hands, closing her eyes, she mentally found herself reciting, "Nevertheless, I am continually with you; You have taken hold of my right hand. You will guide me with your counsel and afterward receive me to glory."

***

She sleeps; alabaster skin caressing the planes of her face, wispy white hair escaping from the hair net and kissing her cheek. Her breathing is so shallow, almost imperceptible. One hundred years of memories swirling in her mind; years of stoically putting one foot in front of the other, facing each day with determination, years of resignation to situations that resisted changes, years of poverty, years of plenty, years when her children brought her joy, years when they brought her sorrow; years of fear when faith in her God was challenged. She that knew although more than ten decades had passed, the breath of God was continually on her face. Had she been asked, she could truthfully have answered, "Never a day passed when I did not have an audience with my Heavenly Father."

Fragments of hymns drift through her mind..."safe in the arms of Jesus, safe, safe"...Then she's a young girl again; running through fields, skirt sculpting her body, pushed by the wind, full of promise of a future. The unwanted cloak of shyness finally gone, a discarded sweater, outgrown, thrown into the air. Safe, safe.... Then she's drawn back again into the present, back to the confines of the bed she knows she will never leave...her mind drifts to this memory, and then that memory. "The one who watches over you will not slumber; indeed He who watches over you never slumbers nor sleeps."

Soon, soon, she feels it in the very marrow of her shrunken body, it won't be long now. In the unseen world, angel wings rustle in anticipation—soon. And then, from the heavenlies, the call comes from the Father, "now, bring my child home; now" A responding whoosh of majestic wings racing down. Her breathing becomes more shallow—"I will never leave you nor forsake you—I will gather you into my arms—I will carry you so your foot will not stumble— even to your old age and gray hair, I am He"—your Father, who loves you, longs for you, and waits to embrace you; and—one last breath—and she's home.

Edith Matthies, October 15, 2007

May All Who Come Behind Us Find Us Faithful [4]

We're pilgrims on the journey
Of the narrow road
And those who've gone before us line the way
Cheering on the faithful, encouraging the weary
Their lives a stirring testament to God's sustaining grace
Surrounded by so great a cloud of witnesses
Let us run the race not only for the prize
But as those who've gone before us
Let us leave to those behind us
The heritage of faithfulness passed on through godly lives

After all our hopes and dreams have come and gone
And our children sift through all we've left behind
May the clues that they discover and the memories they uncover
Become the light that leads them to the road we each must find
To obey! Oh may all who come behind us find us faithful!
May the fire of our devotion light their way
May the footprints that we leave
Lead them to believe
And the lives we live inspire them to obey

Oh may all who come behind us find us faithful
May the fire of our devotion light their way
May the footprints that we leave
Lead them to believe
And the lives we live inspire them to obey.
Oh may all who come behind us find us faithful.

4   http://www.lyricsmode.com/lyrics/s/steve_green/find_us_faithful.html

ACKNOWLEDGEMENTS

Many, many people have invested of themselves into my journey. They have allowed me to examine their lives, have shared vulnerably with me, or have dipped their strong shoulder toward me as we walked through life. Without their transparency, their willingness to mentor and their readiness to teach me, these pages would certainly not have become a reality. What I have observed and learned has come to me as a gift, served on the platter of daily life. Reminiscing fills me with deep gratitude.

~ As to the genesis of this book, I am indebted to my life-mate, Ben and my children who, not only insured I had a story to tell, but tenaciously insisted my thoughts should be recorded for posterity.

This memoir is dedicated to them.

~ Thank you to all those on my Christmas list who plowed through my reflections year after year and still encouraged me to write.

~ Thank you, Denny Smith, my editor. You enthusiastically shared your literary passion, spending many hours patiently tutoring me. A wordsmith, Denny vehemently insisted that my voice should not be lost in the telling of my story, while being equally determined to maintain the integrity of the English language.

~ Thank you, John Zacharias, you caught my mental picture of the book cover and made it a reality.

~ Breanna Dueck Froese, thank you for faithfully reproducing the graphics I envisioned; you are a young woman with great potential.

ABOUT THE AUTHOR

Edith Adrian Matthies was born and grew up in the little farming community of Rosemary, on the Southern Alberta prairie. She and her husband Ben have lived most of their fifty years of marriage in central British Columbia, in the thriving community of Williams Lake. Together they have raised three sons, and have grown a successful family business. She has been committed to the local Mennonite church where she has served in a wide range of leadership as well as teaching roles. Edith is a lover of books, book clubs, and writers groups. **Come Walk With Me, A Life Lived With Joy** is her first book.

Printed in Canada